Tatiana S. Rowson, Kelly Sloan
Personal Leadership in the Age of No Reti

De Gruyter Transformative Thinking and Practice of Leadership and Its Development

Edited by
Bernd Vogel

Volume 7

Tatiana S. Rowson, Kelly Sloan

Personal Leadership in the Age of No Retirement

—

DE GRUYTER

ISBN 978-3-11-131444-0
e-ISBN (PDF) 978-3-11-131614-7
e-ISBN (EPUB) 978-3-11-131634-5
ISSN 2701-4002

Library of Congress Control Number: 2024947337

Bibliographic information published by the Deutsche Nationalbibliothek
The Deutsche Nationalbibliothek lists this publication in the Deutsche Nationalbibliografie;
detailed bibliographic data are available on the internet at http://dnb.dnb.de.

www.degruyter.com
Questions about General Product Safety Regulation:
productsafety@degruyterbrill.com

Advance Praise for *Personal Leadership in the Age of No Retirement*

I well recall, as a journalist and campaigner, writing about later life employment back at the start of the 2000s, when it was something of a "new thing". Then, it was about persuading companies to follow the lead of pioneering businesses like B&Q and tap into the life skills and energy of people in their 50s, 60s and beyond at a time when redundancy programmes systematically culled older staff first, and retirement at a default age could be compulsory.

It was uphill work, and gaining any sort of traction seemed glacial.

How, thankfully, times have changed. Now (through necessity as much as enlightenment) there is a recognition that individuals, organisations and the wider economy benefit through extending working lives.

But how do we convert attitudinal change into meaningful action at a time when employment figures in later life have stalled or even gone backwards?

Clearly, there is still a huge job to do to reset the workplace as somewhere that older people can thrive and continue contributing, and this book puts several important building blocks in place... not least the role leaders need to play within organisations, and how a shift in how individuals themselves view work and their identity within the workplace can make a difference.

This is an exhaustive piece of research delivered in clear language that makes a huge contribution to the massive social need to extend working lives by furthering our understanding of the drivers and mechanisms that can make it possible.

Highly commended reading!

Tony Watts OBE

Longer lives lived will mean longer lives worked. In an age where there will be no retirement, people will have two options: take control and work in a capacity that suits your personal needs, values and motivations or get stuck in a situation which doesn't. This book teaches you the foundations to be CEO of SELF Inc. A book for the intellectually curious, it will guide you through relevant research, asks you questions you need to answer, gives you exercises to explore and it will help you construct healthier foundations for the future. If you're going to work for longer, make sure that time is spent wisely.

Lucy Standing
Founder, Brave Starts

Sometimes you come across a book that speaks directly to you, and to the age. This is such a book. With an ageing global population and an ageing workforce, individuals and organisations need to press the reset button on what life and work look like past 65. Rowson and Sloan have produced a superb contribution to the field, which asks the

https://doi.org/10.1515/9783111316147-202

right questions and offers answers: Important, intelligent and insightful, an essential read.

Prof Jonathan Passmore
Henley Business School, UK

I was intrigued by the ideas in this book. In *Personal Leadership in the Age of No Retirement*, Dr. Tatiana S. Rowson and Dr. Kelly Sloan delve into the emerging phase of life where the concept of retirement is being redefined. As we live longer and healthier lives, this book explores how this new stage impacts work, health, and personal growth.

The authors present a sustainable leadership model that encourages individuals to rethink their career paths and adopt a more fluid approach to integrating work and life. With a mix of scientific insights and practical strategies, this guide is essential for those looking to navigate this transformative era.

Rowson and Sloan leverage their expertise in personal development to offer a new resource for anyone aiming to take new, fascinating, directions in their lives, where the boundaries of work and retirement continue to blur.

Jonathan Foster-Pedley
Board Chair, Association of African Business Schools

Personal Leadership in the Age of No Retirement is an exceptional book for anyone contemplating their next chapter in life. It inspires and challenges conventional views of retirement by presenting robust frameworks for those seeking meaningful careers and fulfilling lives after 65. Tatiana Rowson and Kelly Sloan skillfully integrate research with practical application, offering readers actionable insights grounded in the latest theories. As you embark on this personal journey, you'll be gently encouraged to examine your own beliefs and assumptions. The book illustrates how individuals can successfully leverage their experiences and passions to create rewarding second acts. *Personal Leadership in the Age of No Retirement* is not just a guide; it's a groundbreaking exploration of the potential that later life careers can offer to individuals and to society.

Annu Matula
Executive Coaching

In this time of living longer and important questions around retirement, we must ask ourselves how to move forward and how we need to act now to be able to move into a society, a work environment, and an economy that is sustainable for many years to come; where people of all ages feel welcome, respected, engaged, fulfilled and challenged. Individuals, organisations and government, at all levels we need to prepare ourselves. The current system and old models may have worked in the past, but it is not the way to move forward.

We not only need to redesign the system but we also all need to take responsibility to redesign our future. A future with constant transition into the next phase of our lives, where we stay active much longer, to be part of the economy, to earn an income for many more years: the age of no retirement. We must take leadership of our own life, to be able to adapt to the inevitable changes we will be facing on the way.

The Sustainable Personal Leadership Model, created by Tatiana and Kelly, will guide more and more people on their journey of continuous transformation and to live a life with no regrets! Great publication and of huge value in this time of increasing longevity!

Ingun Bol-de Bock
Creator of Wize Move Society, the online community
for the over50 where we connect, share, learn, evolve and create!

Tatiana and Kelly bring a wealth of knowledge and practical insights to the increasingly important topic of sustainable personal leadership. Their approach recognises that longevity requires not just a change in how we think about retirement, but a fundamental shift in how we lead our lives and careers. The book offers a refreshing and comprehensive perspective, combining rigorous academic research with accessible, practical strategies designed for the reader to take ownership of their development.

Through their focus on personal leadership, Tatiana and Kelly challenge traditional notions of career progression and retirement, advocating for a more flexible, self-directed approach. This aligns closely with the values we promote at Henley Business School, where personal development is a cornerstone of our educational philosophy.

Personal Leadership in the Age of No Retirement is an essential read for anyone looking to navigate the complexities of a longer working life with purpose and resilience. I highly recommend it to professionals and educators alike.

Dr Chris Dalton
Associate Professor of Management Learning
Henley Business School

Acknowledgements

We would like to thank our families – Jeremy, Anna, Lucia and Isabel, and Doug, Emma and Leah – for putting up with us while we wrote this book. And for being pretty fabulous.

Special thanks go to all of the students and participants who have attended our workshops over the years. You have enriched our thinking and have made our experience of facilitating personal leadership development both enjoyable and meaningful.

We would also like to acknowledge our colleagues at Henley Business School. In particular, Chris Dalton set the stage for making personal development a keystone of the Henley MBA and encouraged us to join the conversation and add our stamp to it. Bernd Vogel believed in this book, and we thank him for his supportive leadership.

Leah Saddy, in her role as copy editor of this book, helped to ensure clarity of thought and word. Emma Saddy provided valuable feedback on the manuscript. We thank both of them for demonstrating that this book is also relevant to 30-somethings.

Finally, we would like to thank the De Gruyter team for their professionalism and support.

https://doi.org/10.1515/9783111316147-203

Foreword

We have something to celebrate!

We are living longer, and the good news is that we are living more of those years in good health. Since I was born in the 1960s, life expectancy at birth in the UK has increased from just over 70 to just over 80, that is an extra 10 years! Advances in medical science and healthier living have seen this trend continue. The Office for National Statistics told us almost 10 years ago that one-in-three babies born today will see their 100th birthday.[1]

Parallel to the trend that has seen increases in longevity, we have also seen birthrates fall over recent decades. The impact is that the demographic pyramid, where we had a large number of young people in society supporting a small number of older people, is starting to look more like a column. Government retirement and benefit systems in the UK and many other countries are coming under increasing financial strain and responsibility is shifting to the individual to take care of themselves.

How we prepare for a 100-year life will require us to fundamentally reexamine how we live, our relationship with work, and what we need to do to achieve financial security over the course of our lives. This may sound scary, but with a little bit of imagination, personal leadership, and social solidarity we can find a way forward that is sustainable, equitable, fulfilling and rewarding.

For generations we have lived our adult lives in three distinct phases: starting with a period of education or training, followed by work, and ending with a few years of retirement. If you use the analogy of life as a journey, we have added our gift of extra years to the end of the motorway without changing any of the on and off ramps that signify different phases of our lives. In my case, you could see it as adding 10 miles to the end of the journey without getting access to any service stations on the last stretch. There is a chance I will run out of petrol or get bored, neither situation is desirable.

We need to reimagine how we will live in the future, so that we can do the things we want in our personal lives, achieve the things that are important to us professionally, and ensure that we have the financial security to make this all work. We will dip in and out of education and work more frequently and at different times of our lives than we have in the past. To do this, we will need to have a clear picture of what is important to us and a roadmap of how we want to achieve this.

We can see responsibility is shifting to the individual when it comes to preparing for retirement; we need to proactively take responsibility for other aspects of our careers and personal lives to make sure that we are creating a sustainable future for ourselves – one where we can achieve our goals and realise our dreams. This book

---

1 https://www.ons.gov.uk/peoplepopulationandcommunity/birthsdeathsandmarriages/lifeexpectan cies/articles/whatareyourchancesoflivingto100/2016-01-14

https://doi.org/10.1515/9783111316147-204

gives us the tools to build our own roadmaps, and the encouragement to experiment and think in new ways.

In the post-war years, the concept of being a teenager developed to describe the years between childhood and adulthood. It reflected cultural shifts that were happening at a time of increased prosperity and were coupled with changes and advancements in the labour market. Arguably, we are going through comparable cultural and technological changes today, but the group impacted are not young adults, but people who are mid-career, those trying to figure out what's next. We have not come up with a term like 'teenager' that will provide these people with the sense of identity that will give them a voice and help them create a movement. Whoever comes up with the name will certainly solve a big challenge for many of us working in the longevity space. That aside, key to helping this group find their way forward and thrive in the future is to help them achieve self-empowerment and sustainable personal leadership.

Mike Mansfield
CEO ProAge

Foreword by the series editor

"Midlife is a particularly good time for us to take control of our trajectories."
– *Personal Leadership in the Age of No Retirement* (2025, p. 42).

Midlife or "new phase of adulthood"! Yes. However, this book is also a wonderful invitation to aim for sustainable personal leadership during our entire life!

"This might not really be a book on leadership ..." Yes it is!

When Tatiana and Kelly approached me with their book idea, they more or less started with: "Well, Bernd, this might not really be a book on leadership, but would you be interested in reading the proposal...?". If leading yourself is not the training, developmental process and resource to lead others and also have others in your sphere benefit from sustainable personal leadership, I don't know what is.

I read *Personal Leadership in the Age of No Retirement* for the first time in full during a period where I was in one of my regular routines of reflecting on my trajectory, working on what Tatiana and Kelly so powerfully call "Self, Inc." The book is infectious. You cannot let go. It is asking in a gentle but also assertive way the questions we might have thought of but formulated differently; questions we know we need to ask but shied away from, because we think they are too complicated, painful or overwhelming, but are actually rewarding and empowering in the authors' language; or questions we were not aware that we should or can ask about ourselves. The book is a great invitation to work on your own trajectories in different spheres of life that all hang together.

To do so introduces and provides a range of concepts, ideas, challenges and tools that help guide you through the phase of midlife or a new stage of adulthood. Even the conversation about how we look differently at our life stages, journeys, trajectories is already a great nudge to shake up one's own perception. Retirement is a relatively new idea. Ageing has often a rather negative connotation. Turning this around to name it an opportunity for "midlife empowerment" that challenges our own biases and blind spots on ageing is a refreshing perspective.

The aspiration to capture "the new midlife", what this can mean and how it is changing, gives the reader practical tools and but also the language to access, learn and grow through these exciting years or decades. While my children call me ancient to wind me up, I will respond in the future by saying I am in a "new phase of adulthood"!

Linking this phase to self-leadership provides the reader agency that many in busy and compressed lives, often perceived as controlled by others, might want to regain based on this book's solid research, experiences and the invitation to work on the book's key ideas and suggestions.

Beyond the focus on people in the phase of adulthood, the ideas and practices in the Sustainable Personal Leadership model are helpful in all phases of life. When

https://doi.org/10.1515/9783111316147-205

does your personal work on purpose, identities, life domains or personal resources really start? The earlier the better.

A book for real challenges and puzzles

This book series is about making a difference and offering solutions to real world problems. What is the point otherwise of having a book series and asking writers and readers to invest their time and energy? And this book is spot on. It tickles and positively irritates you because you know very well that it is time to explore and lead your personal trajectory.

The way Tatiana and Kelly have designed the book makes it also actionable. It is difficult not to start reflecting, not to start working on the activities in the book, and not to draw conclusions as you go along. And that is the sign of a relevant and impactful book.

Personal Leadership in the Age of No Retirement is your book if you aim to strengthen your ability to change and adapt yourself and your lives proactively and in response to new aspirations and realities. How about becoming a stronger activist and less a bystander for your own destiny? In turn, this will have generative ripple effects for other lives in your vicinity. If we dial forward 10 years, I am keen to learn to whom, how and why this book made a difference. I am more than certain it will.

While my own conversations and struggles of recalibration continue ..., Tatiana and Kelly, thank you for bringing this exciting book to the series. We would have a huge gap without your work.

Bernd Vogel
Henley-on-Thames, UK
September 2024

Contents

Part I: **The background for personal leadership**

Chapter 4
The new midlife —— **36**

Part II: **Personal leadership in action**

Chapter 5
Self-awareness —— **51**

Chapter 6
Professional identity —— **68**

Part I: **The background for personal leadership**

ised and fluid, personal agency and leadership are essential enablers of positive outcomes.

Increased life expectancy does not only affect us at an individual level. This is a global phenomenon that is not showing any signs of reversing. Instead, we see more and more countries faced with an unprecedented demographic shift. While there has been a surge of books and publications discussing the challenges and opportunities associated with this demographic shift, there has not been as much emphasis on how personal leadership development models should be updated to reflect the realities of a longer adulthood.

To our knowledge, most personal leadership models and literature in use today are directly derived from 20th century parameters and insights. In the past five years, there has been unprecedented social change associated with major events such as the global COVID-19 pandemic, climate change, political transitions, war, and migration. These had a direct impact on how we, as individuals, think about work and how organisations think about us as workers. Some academic research has started to explore possible approaches, but these rarely reach a wider audience. In writing this book, we aim to present a personal leadership development approach that is fit for purpose in the era of increased longevity. A model that is flexible, inclusive, and sustainable.

Our 'sustainable personal leadership' model, although designed to be practical and actionable, is grounded in academic research. We build on Tatiana's research interest in midlife transitions, ageing and well-being at work and Kelly's in language, personal leadership and lifelong learning. In addition, we each have personal experience of making career changes, some painful or difficult, but nonetheless not impossible and often ultimately rewarding. We have both lived and worked in multiple countries and have adapted to new environments, new realities, opportunities and roadblocks. Thus, our model and our thinking on this topic are enriched by our own lived experiences.

We are also informed by our expertise in facilitating personal leadership development of professionals, managers, and executives. Individuals in our workshops or coaching practice are often experiencing mid-career or midlife dilemmas and decisions. Despite the multitude of books on leadership, career transitions, wellness and well-being, we could not find a book that could capture personal leadership for 21st century lives. From our frustration came the idea to write our own model that can guide one's personal leadership development with longer lives in mind. Our model can be used by individuals or as part of a coaching programme.

1.1 CEO of Self, Inc.

While personal leadership may be an idea we are unfamiliar with, most of us have an intuitive concept of leadership. For example, we all will likely have an image of what a good CEO looks like. They will have a vision of the future. They will be able to tell a

Chapter 1
Introduction

When we first came up with the idea of writing this book, we shared the view that current approaches to personal leadership are disconnected from the realities of 21st century life. Today we live longer, and often healthier, lives than ever before. This is the first time in history that this is becoming a common occurrence, not an exception. A consequence of this longer life expectancy is that a new life stage is emerging between early and late adulthood. This phenomenon is similar to how in the 20th century adolescence emerged as a distinct life stage, situated between childhood and adulthood. Therefore, although we are living longer, adulthood does not simply stretch out. For example: In our 50s and 60s, we are unlikely to have the same energy levels than we had in our 30s while at the same time we might have acquired far more emotional resilience. Therefore, it is logical to think that our relationships with our work, with the jobs we do and with the roles we desire will change as we move into mid and late adulthood. This is what makes this book very exciting; it is a call for action so we can shape this new life stage as a time of meaningful opportunities.

Working for longer is clearly important to sustain our increased life span. This is not necessarily something negative. If we consider the premise that work is a source of fulfilment, then the idea of being able to continue for longer begins to sound like something we should aspire to. The way we tend to think about retirement is grounded in how this life stage developed in the 20th century and it is connected to increased industrialisation and the emergence of social systems. As we will discuss in Chapter 2, much has changed since. Not only in terms of our life expectancy, but in the way our society operates today. This means that the way we work and live has changed to an extent that old models of career and retirement are no longer useful. These models now have simply historical value. Therefore, we will be building on 'the age of no retirement' movement (Collie, 2015) to introduce the idea of *engaged retirement*. This does not imply that retirement will no longer exist, but rather that the nature of retirement is changing and does not necessarily mean disengagement from work and other social roles.

In this new era of increased longevity, we will often be required to recalibrate our goals and activities as we grow older. While career and life reinventions are not new, it is the fact that these transitions will be a norm that is challenging. There are no established pathways or roles for this new stage of adulthood. There is also not a formula that will work well for everyone. This means that we will need to rely on our personal leadership to drive our lives with purpose as we shape our version of engaged retirement. We are not saying that governments, organisations, and society do not also have a responsibility in creating the conditions (and opportunities) for us to thrive. Instead, we are emphasising that as our lives become increasingly individual-

https://doi.org/10.1515/9783111316147-001

story, to articulate what the company is and where it is going, and how to get there. This will involve understanding of its past, of its resources, of its strengths and weaknesses, and of its purpose. They will try to balance short-term and long-term goals. They will have a clear sense of the values the company stands by. They will have a team of people who manage different aspects of the organisation and they will have good working relationships with these individuals and open communication between themselves and the teams, and also across teams. They will have a strategy for how to allocate resources across the company. They will have a style, an approach to leading that works for them, a way of feeling and being authentic in their skin, while making decisions which effect the entire company and have ramifications across the whole.

Now, what if we imagine that you, the individual, are at one and the same time, an organisation (like the company in the above example) and also the leader of that organisation; in essence, you are the CEO of 'Self, Inc.'. As the leader, you envision a goal, determine the values, make strategic decisions, and work with a team (in this case, the team may include different aspects of self) to allocate resources. Pushing this metaphor, we can see that as the leader, the well-being and sustainability of Self, Inc. are dependent on you making good leadership decisions. For the 'company' to be successful, you need to have a vision for the future; a set of values; an understanding of your resources and how sustainable these are; and an ability to allocate resources in a way that promotes the health and well-being of the whole person. In short, you need self-awareness coupled with good leadership skills.

We do an exercise in our MBA workshops where we ask participants to draw a metaphor of their career. Some years ago, a participant in one of our workshops, Mark, drew an eye-catching image. It was a picture of a hand holding and manipulating the strings of a marionette. Mark described his feeling of not being in control of his career, of having decisions made for him by others, of having no personal agency. We asked, 'What if you were the hand, and not the puppet? How could you make that happen?' It is this kind of personal agency that we are proposing here, which is an inherent aspect of personal leadership.

None of us are surprised by the notion that organisations need leadership, so why should we be surprised by the fact that we, as individuals, benefit from good personal leadership as well? And that this leadership comes from within? We are each ultimately in charge of making the decisions that affect the sustainable health and well-being of our own selves, so it makes sense to approach these decisions as a good leader would, being aware of the resources at our disposal, the changing context that we live in, and the goals that we strive towards. Note that this is not about being self-centred or selfish. The decisions that we make affect us, but they also ripple out to everyone around us; looking after ourselves is the first step in being able to function in a healthy way in our multiple identities and contexts – as individuals, as workers, and as members of family and social networks.

1.2 Sustainable personal leadership model

We define *sustainable personal leadership* as the ability to change and adapt ourselves and our lives in response to new aspirations and realities. Personal leadership is a process, rather than a state. It involves self-awareness, contextual awareness, reflection and action. Although in the literature there is no established definition for personal leadership, we chose this term because it gives us the freedom to integrate different areas of knowledge to make sense of this new longer working life.

Our sustainable personal leadership model is the map, or a mapped-out process, to gain and maintain personal leadership fit for longer lives (see Figure 1.1). So, it is designed to improve our ability to change and adapt ourselves and our lives in response to new aspirations and realities. This is grounded on three core steps: purpose, alignment and experimentation.

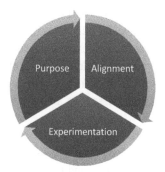

Figure 1.1: Sustainable Personal Leadership Model.

1.2.1 Purpose

At the heart of personal leadership is purpose. We cannot move forward, or move anywhere meaningful without clear intent. There is a difference between reactive movement versus proactive movement; we can move without a vision if we are only moving reactively. It is proactive movement that is purposeful. The question 'what is your purpose?' is often a difficult one to answer. When we run workshops, people find it difficult to articulate. For some, the idea of purpose seems off-putting and overwhelming because it links to an idea of 'grand purpose'. In our sustainable personal leadership model, this should not be seen as something too far from everyday life. It is linked to understanding ourselves holistically and as working people; and we can only place ourselves in the right place if we have self and contextual awareness. Purpose means knowing who we are and how best to communicate that in the context of our lives and work. It involves looking back and evaluating our biographies and narratives. We sub-divide this into two areas of exploration: self-awareness (Chapter 5) and professional identity (Chapter 6).

Understanding ourselves involves a journey of discovery to recognise those events, experiences, and people which have influenced our self-concept, actions and decisions. In undergoing this process, we may find that certain truths we hold may no longer be valid or relevant. This is especially the case when we start separating who we are from social expectations we may live by without questioning (Chapter 5). Understanding who we are allows us to make informed decisions that enable us to feel more aligned and inevitably more fulfilled. We call this having an inside-out orientation or mindset as opposed to an outside-in one that is dictated by others (we will refer to these two orientations throughout the book). Our sense of self, however, is not fixed. It is continuously being shaped by our life experiences. This is why we emphasise the idea of recalibration as an on-going process.

The second aspect within the theme of purpose is our professional identity. Although it is linked to self-concept, it refers to how we present and frame who we are for a particular market, the job market. A professional brand is also malleable, so it is not only bound to change as our sense of self evolves but is also framed according to changes in our context. There is a clear hierarchy here, because we can only talk about a strong professional identity once we have worked out who we are. Otherwise, we will spend a lifetime presenting a brand others assigned to us. One of the major challenges people in midlife face is when they notice their sense of self has changed, but they find it difficult to translate this as a coherent professional narrative with what came before. This is quite important in the process of recalibration; we do not throw away anything, but repurpose, re-frame and expand in a way that leads to more meaningful work. These two aspects of purpose allow us to navigate life with our eyes wide open, conscious of what matters to us and having a framework to evaluate and make sustainable decisions.

1.2.2 Alignment

This aspect makes personal leadership sustainable. Alignment allows us to move forward by focusing on what matters, and, more importantly, to do so without depleting ourselves. As we go through life, we develop different identities associated with the roles we play or groups where we belong. Over time, we may grow out of certain identities or we may find that others are no longer viable, either because we realise they are living according to the expectations of others, or because our priorities have changed. So, it happens that we find ourselves out of alignment. When we align our purpose with the various roles we play in different life domains, we are able to be more focused and eliminate activities and areas that do not offer any rewards. Inevitably this is a second step in our model because it depends on understanding our purpose first. We divided alignment into two aspects: life domains (Chapter 7) and resources (Chapter 8).

Life domains refer to our social roles, e.g., daughter, wife, author, teacher, and relevant life domains, e.g., family, work, learning and development, exercise and nutrition, etc. These roles and domains are uniquely defined by us and go beyond the simple work-life (out of work) dyad we usually see featured in conversations about work-life balance. We are the only ones who can define what aspects of life are relevant to us at any given time. Moreover, only we can judge which of these domains or roles are essential to our identity, desirable or no longer necessary. This means that we have the power to deploy our investment in terms of energy and attention to what brings us the most reward. It is not unusual that our workshop participants realise that a portion of their time is wasted in areas of no consequence and realise that they need to let go of them to free themselves to do more meaningful things. Selecting areas and domains of importance is key to ageing well and achieving a sustainable career as we live longer.

Resources is the next aspect of this step in our model and it refers to the bank of resources, e.g., social, psychological, that we have accumulated to be deployed as needed. Our resource levels impact on our ability to cope with everyday demands, as well as our readiness to respond to opportunities or challenges that may emerge. It is linked to the domains and roles explored in the previous aspect and may be stretched thin if we are less focused on what matters. This is why it is so important to revise our life domains to ensure we are not wasting resources which could be used elsewhere. Resources are not unlimited; neither are they a matter of luck or chance. So, while it is important to actively monitor our resource levels, there are effective ways to keep them well stocked.

1.2.3 Experimentation

The final step in our personal leadership model is experimentation. This stage can be fun and intimidating at the same time and there is no way we can recalibrate if we do not test our purpose and alignment in practice. There are two aspects to experimentation: action and reflection (which are both discussed in Chapter 9).

Action involves trying out changes, and making adjustments from the insights we have achieved so far. Making a change can be daunting, and this is the value of experimenting, trying out new ways of being and doing. Experiments can be large or small, and can take place in safe environments, in our imagination, or in our usual contexts. Depending on the magnitude of what we need to recalibrate, we may need time to get a good feel of how it works for us. Here it is important to note that the process of changing and shifting is inherent to being human and taking an active role in this developmental cycle can be very empowering, especially as we develop a benign curiosity and confidence in managing ourselves, our priorities, and our resources. Like the agile approach to project management, action also allows us to incorporate other adjustments as we get a sense of how our vision works in practice.

Finally, and closely linked to action, comes reflection. Reflection can be in action, in the moment, to allow us to make smaller adjustments or manage unexpected events. There is also a need to engage in deeper reflection to evaluate our purpose and alignment, and perhaps set up another cycle of recalibration and learning. A new cycle that allows us to lead ourselves through the next stretch, sustainably and meaningfully.

1.3 Our approach to development

When considering personal leadership, we immediately think about 'development'. Just as we note in the theories we introduce here, 'development' is an accepted term to describe moving on from one stage to another successfully, and hopefully as a better, more integrated, person. We do, however, have an issue with the assumption that development implies a linear progression. Maybe that is related to all these different theories and models that are presented in progressive order without necessarily representing the multitude of unique options and paths available to us. This is especially important when we consider our longer lives. Because as we age, development is also an adjustment to new realities. It requires adaptability and flexibility to learn new, different ways to be ourselves. So, we will continue using the word 'development', as this is an established term. But there is a caveat. When we talk of development, we would like you to think in terms of recalibration.

Recalibration reflects much better the spirit (and logic) of process needed from midlife onwards (see Chapter 4). Instead of linear, progressive development (e.g., the idea of a career ladder), we should be looking into making changes, learning in a way that refreshes what we do for a better fit with our needs, wants, capabilities and resources (e.g., learning cycles). Therefore, this is not a matter of better or worse, but a different approach that will work well for the next stretch, until we need to recalibrate again.

Recalibration means to calibrate again, so in order to understand the term, we need to look at the meaning of calibration. This word usually refers to scientific measurement. Calibration involves comparison or standardisation against a fixed reference point. When we calibrate an instrument, we ensure its accuracy by comparing it to specific standards. We might think of this as the 'narrow' definition of calibrate. However, it also means 'to change the way you do or think about something' (Cambridge University Press, n.d: online). We can think of this as the 'broad' definition.

For our purposes, this broader definition is more interesting. It has to do with changing our frames of reference and/or our behaviours. To make this clear, let's look at some of the synonyms of recalibration:

> adjust, amend, change, develop, modify, reshape, revamp, revise, shift, transform, vary, adapt, alter, analyse, annotate, arrange, assemble.

Thus 'recalibration' has both a narrow, specific, scientific meaning, and a broader meaning which is expanded and applied to frames of thinking. Notice these synonyms: 'reshape, revamp, shift, transform'. They suggest not the very small shifts in measurement that are used to calibrate, say, a thermometer or a scale, but rather they represent foundational changes in perception. Recalibration in this sense is a shake-up; applied to personal leadership it changes our perception of where we sit in the grand scheme of things. The scale may still be small: we can recalibrate by making small adjustments, but the context is larger. Note that these synonyms also imply action; when we recalibrate, we set a new path and new directions. This broader meaning of recalibration is still based in the concepts of measurement and of comparison, but less so with standardisation. This is because standardisation requires a fixed reference point, while here we allow the reference points to shift.

As an example, let's look at the changes to our attitudes and behaviours around work that resulted from the COVID-19 pandemic, with its accompanying lockdowns and restrictions on travel. Many of us switched from working in an office to working at home during this time. This involved a recalibration, a shift in where the boundaries were between work and home, and how we handled personal space, family space, time, technology, and communication. You may now be recalibrating again by trying hybrid working, or some other model of working. There are likely to be many more recalibrations of our attitudes towards where and how we work as we move forward; but it is clear that a big shift has occurred in our expectations and priorities which may never return to pre-COVID realities. While the pandemic was a global event which caused societal changes around the nature of work, most examples of recalibration will be smaller and more personal. Parenting requires recalibration, for example. So does moving; when you move companies or countries you need to recalibrate to the norms and expectations of new social groups and cultures.

The model that we propose understands 'development' similarly to the idea of recalibration and lifelong learning. Sustainable personal leadership decisions take place throughout the cycle and in multiple iterations of the cycle; these decisions 'reshape, revamp, shift, transform' our conceptions of self and our identities.

1.4 How the book is organised

This book is organised into two parts. The first is theoretical and the second is practical, although you will find that this description is too vague, as there is practice in the theory and theory in the practice. You can easily start at the beginning and read your way through. Alternatively, you may find yourself dipping into it, and reading it in a less structured way. Or reading through it quickly, and then going back to work your way through some of the chapters in more depth.

The first part contains four chapters, which put the book into a contextual and theoretical framework. Chapter 1 (this one) introduces our model, defines some of the terms and concepts we use, and discusses why we felt the book was needed in the first place. It is a topic we feel strongly about and we try to ground it in both our personal lived experiences and our professional expertise. In the remaining chapters of this section, we present some of the demographic realities behind the need to re-think retirement, and explore the theoretical underpinnings of adult development, ageing, career, and ageing at work, and about the language and social biases that underlie discussions of ageing. This is all part of the context of midlife career changes, looked at from the viewpoints of demographics, policy, legislation, culture, psychology, and sociology.

In *Part II* of the book, we will work through some very practical exercises to increase your self-awareness and to reflect on how you can utilise leadership skills in the strategic decision making necessary to ensure your well-being and a sustainable future for an engaged retirement. In these chapters, we will examine how you make sense of self, your professional identity, and your resources. We will encourage you to experiment and give you ideas for action, as well as for reflection. These chapters utilise many exercises and pose reflexive questions. We encourage you to write things down; utilise a journal or a file to keep your thoughts. You will get more from the book if you take the time to do the exercises and answer the questions. But, as with recalibration in general, this can be an iterative process; you may find that the book works best for you in large doses or small ones. There is no wrong way to approach the book. The chapters in Part II, and the exercises and examples therein, are intended to get you thinking, and to flex your personal leadership muscles, so that you are in a position to provide strong and thoughtful strategies for yourself moving forward. The final chapter closes the book with some reflections on what personal leadership is really about and how to take it forward.

Chapter 2
Theoretical foundations of 'personal leadership'

In our many years of delivering workshops and working with professionals and executives reaching midlife, it has become clear to us that this stage in life is complex and cannot be truly explored without a holistic perspective. At this stage of our lives, we know that it is impossible to compartmentalise work, family, health and well-being, etc., as separate entities. Quite the contrary, the influence from one domain to another is evident in the stories and conversations we have with 'midlifers' at our workshops or through our research. In this chapter, we will draw our ideas from a few key areas of research and practice to conceptualise our notion of *personal leadership* as a sustainable approach to our longevity and engaged retirement.

2.1 Career conversations

Careers research and practice is a vast area of knowledge that sometimes does not communicate well with other areas of personal and professional development. It is not unusual to have a picture in our minds of the school career counsellor evaluating what subjects we are good at and what career we should follow based on that. Both of us have met a multitude of accountants, engineers and finance professionals who were good at maths in school and this defined their first career choice (not necessarily their second or third career). Despite how recognisable this approach to careers is, this is not by any means a representation of the research and practice in this area. Career is a complex topic; it covers several life stages, transitions in and out of education, the dynamics between work and other roles, organisational development, career change and exit from workforce. We will address this topic more practically in Chapter 6. But before we get there, there are a few key insights that inform how we developed our *Sustainable personal leadership* model.

Work forms a big part of our overall identity and it is natural that we feel the need to align with other aspects of identity and our values. In Tatiana's own research (see Rowson et al., 2021) on cross-domain career transitions, it became clear that misalignment between our careers and our other life domains can happen as we take on or withdraw from different social roles (e.g., become a parent, support the career of our partner). A mismatch leads to a sense of discomfort and dissatisfaction that over time can become unsustainable. An example of this is when a person who has a role that involves frequent travelling and time away from the family also has caring responsibilities. The two may be reconcilable in practice with hired help, or with a network of support. Or, despite the solutions available, it may still create an internal conflict for them. This would drive them to make changes. Only the person can tell if roles and identities are congruent or not, because for the outside observer everything

https://doi.org/10.1515/9783111316147-002

may seem fine. We will explore how this can be addressed in practice in the second part of this book.

We all understand the financial aspects of work, we are reminded in our workshops every time that work and income generation are closely linked. However, meaningful work plays an important role in our motivation, engagement and well-being. In fact, there is research into the detrimental impact of meaningless jobs (see Graeber, 2018). In our workshops, when we introduce the careers conversation, we always set the scene with a popular parable of the wandering scholar, as told below.

Once upon a time, on a sunny morning, a medieval scholar known for his wisdom and inquisitive nature arrived in a quaint village. He decided to take a stroll through the village and enjoy the serene beauty of the countryside. As he wandered along, he came across a construction site where four men were hard at work. Intrigued by the scene, the scholar approached the first worker and inquired, 'What are you doing?' The man, with a weary expression, replied, 'I am laying bricks, sir.' Aware that one perspective was insufficient, the scholar moved on to the second worker and posed the same question, 'What are you doing?' The second worker, slightly more enthusiastic, responded, 'I am building a wall, sir.' With a sense of anticipation, the scholar continued to the third worker, who was busy humming a joyful tune as he worked with passion and dedication. The scholar asked once more, 'And what are you doing?' The third worker paused, looked up at the vast sky above, and then, with a radiant smile, replied, 'I am building a cathedral, sir!' Finally, the scholar approached the last man in that section of the building site and posed the same question. The man looked the scholar in the eye and said, 'I am working to bring food and shelter to my beloved family.' The scholar was taken aback by the contrasting responses he had received from these men who were, after all, engaged in the same task. He realised that their different interpretations of their work reflected their unique perspectives and attitudes towards life.

This story demonstrates that the meaning and fulfilment one derives from one's work are deeply influenced by one's perspective, attitudes and perceptions. Just like these workers, we can choose to see our daily tasks as simply chores, as contributions to a larger goal, as integral parts of a grand vision that can inspire and motivate you, or as an act of love. It is important to note that none of these is right or wrong, but one may be right for any one person at a particular time, and a perception that may seem to be right, or better, from an outside observer may be wrong for the person. This is an individual choice, and it can profoundly affect our satisfaction and sense of purpose in our career and life. Therefore, as individuals we are central to our career experiences and the meanings we attach to them. In the careers literature there is a clear consensus on the importance of the person in their work outcomes and experience of success. Therefore, career development and decisions inevitably should be dictated by the person, from the inside out.

2.1.1 Inside-out career orientation

This idea of an 'inside out' career focus is echoed by many careers authors. Mark Savickas who is a thought leader in the field with research and practical experience, argues that we should take an active role in constructing our careers. We will be building on Savickas' ideas in this book a few times. He developed the career construction theory and an approach to career counselling called 'life design' that helps individuals to align their careers with their values, interests and skills to achieve a fulfilling and meaningful working life (see Savickas et al., 2009; Savickas, 2020). As part of this, he discusses the role of personal narratives and the importance of taking control of our past and present narrative to realise our career potential and aspirations. This is not to say that a person should make up a random story about themselves and see if that materialises. Unfortunately, there is no magic. What he says instead is that we should purposefully reflect on the meaningful aspects of our lives and align them with our narratives. This is achieved by being conscious of our identities and stories, and by making sense of how we are attaching meaning to our experiences. It is not unusual to find that we are constructing our stories in the automatic pilot, and that we are missing important aspects, or simply repeating patterns from others, e.g., family or social groups. For instance, when a person gets a highly paid job that may involve tasks that are against one's personal values, or accepts a promotion to a role that, although prestigious or good on paper, takes away the fulfilling aspect of the job (and the reason one got into it in the first place). We call this the curse of common-sense career choices. Conversely, when we are active in constructing our career, aware of our personal narratives, we are more effective in making choices and decisions that are more likely to lead to meaningful and fulfilling work.

The emphasis on the person as the agent in their career is stressed in the work of two key authors: Michael Arthur and Douglas Hall. They both gained prominence in the late 1990s for two distinct, yet aligned, theories. Arthur and his colleagues (see Arthur & Rousseau, 1996) introduced the notion of a boundaryless career, which is a career approach that goes beyond organisational, industry or national boundaries. In essence, boundaryless means free from constraints and limitations associated with traditional career paths. While at the time this was a groundbreaking idea, now it's quite common to think about careers in those terms. In the post pandemic world, with the emergence of remote and hybrid work, the idea of boundarylessness was expanded even further to a career beyond the office space, making this theory more current than ever. One main aspect of this new, boundaryless, career landscape is that opportunities can be pursued beyond one's current employment or occupation. So, working people may have a greater pool of possibilities they can explore. For example, John started his career working in company X in product design. Over the years, he could have migrated to a different company or sector, or moved countries or even changed roles. According to the boundaryless career theory, he is not constrained by his starting point. In fact, moving around becomes a good strategy to develop in his career.

Consistent with this scenario is the premise that one should take responsibility for their own career. In practice this means that we must ensure we have career goals, that we have the right knowledge, skills and connections and our professional profile is attractive outside and inside the organisation. Arthur refers to many of these aspects as 'career capital' individuals should acquire, nurture and when needed spend. Therefore, just as emphasised by Savickas, to thrive in our career we need to be taking the lead by being active and not passive.

The second theory, developed by Hall and colleagues (see Hall, 1996; 2004) is called a protean career. Named after the Greek god Proteus, who was known for his shapeshifting abilities, this concept emphasises the idea of flexibility and adaptability. A protean career, like boundaryless, stresses the importance of proactive careers management beyond organisational constraints. The rationale for this approach to careers, however, is internally driven rather than contextual. Career decisions and moves are motivated by individual fulfilment rather than a more flexible landscape of work. Personal values and self-direction are important aspects helping individuals navigate career choices and goals. Hall suggests that this type of career orientation requires a clear self-concept and ability to adapt and change to keep work aligned with one's values and sense of self (see also Denyer & Rowson, 2022). A good example is when individuals leave an organisation job to retrain as a teacher or to work for a cause or an NGO. These values don't necessarily need to be societal values, but can be attached to one's personal development. For example, Suki left her job as a headhunter because the excessive travelling and the long hours were incompatible with a family life. She had no intention to have a career break, but wanted to be there at dinner time, to put her children to bed and attend school concerts. Although she was very well paid, her work slowly became more and more meaningless. Changing jobs to something more aligned with her values became inevitable.

Any theory receives some level of scepticism. Protean was particularly criticised for being only achievable by people who are in a position of privilege who can afford to put their personal values and fulfilment above an income or job security. Similar criticism was placed on the emphasis on job mobility implied by the boundaryless career theory. These points are not unfounded, given that much of the research on both career approaches derived from MBA graduates, who by default would have greater resources to drive their career in their own terms. Yet, when we look at all these ideas together, we can see a trend towards an approach to career development that is dynamic and requires self-awareness, proactivity and adaptability.

2.1.2 Sustainable career development

Another insight that our model borrows from careers literature is the concept of sustainable careers introduced by De Vos and colleagues (2020). Building on ageing literature, this approach considers the relationship between people-organisations and the wider system across the life course. It explores how various factors may interact to impact work outcomes over time. Thus, discerning what can hinder or help someone stay at work for longer, sustainably. For example, reskilling and keeping up with technology trends so as not to be out of date, or ensuring that stress levels are not too high or no injury is incurred at work or elsewhere that can affect health and functioning in the long term.

De Vos and colleagues' view is that careers should mutually benefit the person as well the wider system, so win-win. They challenge the view that people are simply replaceable, and argue that if we look after workers so they are healthy and skilled enough, their contribution to society and organisations is sustainable. This is very aligned with the view from ageing research and policy makers (see Chapter 3), that longer working lives are not simply linked to an increased longevity, but also linked to the possibility of enjoying a fulfilling and healthy longer life.

De Vos and colleagues, similarly to ageing well experts, champion the idea of self-regulation and dynamic learning. When we are able to reflect and understand the impact of positive and negative experiences, we have the opportunity to learn and adapt our choices as our careers progress. We become more consciously aware of ourselves, our personal and work environments, and the job market. This ongoing process helps us continuously improve our understanding of how we fit into our career path over time. Sustainability is not a static state to be achieved, but a dynamic equilibrium to be mastered through some level of recalibration. Our needs and wants will likely change as we age, so what worked for us in our 30s is unlikely to work into our 70s. Adjustments and tweaks to different aspects of life are key to retaining choices that are meaningful to us.

A good example of how our preferences change over time is business travel. For instance, John found business travel to be exciting and fulfilling for many years and was quick to volunteer for roles that involved travel. He was famous for flying overnight and arriving in shape for a 9 a.m. meeting where he was giving a presentation. This was one of his superpowers. At some point, as he grew older, travelling lost much of its appeal, becoming a chore, and John found that he could not be asked to sacrifice his sleep or comfort. As his needs and wants changed, John found it made sense to give these kinds of opportunities to others in his team. This did not diminish his leadership. Felicity, on the other hand, passed over many opportunities to travel for business when the children were young. When childcare responsibilities were no longer an impediment, her priorities changed and she saw herself putting her hand up for business travel opportunities within her team. In one year, she went abroad at least 15 times.

Sustainable careers, unlike the boundaryless, protean or life-design approaches, focuses also on organisations and society at large. So, the authors argue for the need to foster an environment in which people can thrive and develop their careers sustainably. This is quite an important point, as without the right conditions it is very challenging to manage our careers sustainably. Although this book is aimed at individuals, we would like you, the reader, to be aware of your role in shaping workplaces that allow others to be productive for longer.

2.2 Adult development

Our model draws on a few key aspects of adult development literature. The pioneers from psychology believed that development happened mainly in childhood and adolescence. A few authors, however, took a different view and theorised about adult development. Many of these theories have since been validated by research evidence or observed in practice.

2.2.1 Jung

One of the first authors to write about adult development was Carl Jung (1960), the Swiss psychiatrist and psychoanalyst. His work focused, among other things, on personal growth throughout adulthood. Individuation, as Jung named it, referred to the lifelong process of psychological development, wherein individuals strive to become their true and authentic selves by integrating conscious and unconscious aspects of the psyche. Jung believed that all individuals naturally seek individuation and this process would largely take place in the second half of life. Jung makes a clear distinction between these two phases of psychological development.

According to Jung, the first half of life is primarily focused on external factors such as education, career, building relationships, and establishing oneself in society. The primary goal is to develop a stable ego and establish a solid foundation for one's life. During this phase, individuals are focused on meeting societal expectations, pursuing success, and fulfilling traditional roles and responsibilities. Therefore, individuals at this stage are motivated by external approval and symbols of success. When we think about our relationship with our work and career, at this stage we would accept a particular job or take on a project because it looks and sounds good. Or is something that others around us find desirable. We see in our workshops many people who made career decisions on this basis without considering their purpose, what they truly want. We say in our workshops that there is nothing wrong with these decisions, or with any lack of fulfilment or satisfaction of not being true to ourselves. Experiencing that is not only important, but it is also a natural part of finding who we are and what is important to us.

The second half of life, often associated with midlife and beyond, represents a shift in focus and priorities. Jung viewed this phase as an opportunity for individuals to reconnect with neglected parts of themselves and engage in a process of self-discovery and individuation. It is a time when individuals confront existential questions, seek deeper meaning and purpose, and explore their inner worlds. Jung argued that one of the central tasks of the second half of life is the integration of the unconscious. This involves acknowledging and coming to terms with repressed aspects of the self, such as shadow elements and unresolved conflicts to achieve a greater sense of wholeness, authenticity, and personal growth. So, according to Jung, midlife brings an important shift in priorities towards authenticity that is crucial for our sense of fulfilment beyond this point. This idea of shift and the difference between these two halves are at the core of sustainable personal leadership development for longer lives.

2.2.2 Erikson

A second author that offers useful insights into adult development is Erik Erikson (1980; 1985). He built on Freud's psychoanalytic theory to develop his theory of psychosocial development. He is renowned for his eight stages of psychosocial development, from infancy to old age. Erikson's view is that each stage of our development is characterised by a certain psychosocial challenge or task that we seek to overcome. These tasks involve reconciling and balancing conflicting psychological and social demands. Resolving each stage of development leads to personal growth and 'healthy personality', as we become equipped to resolve subsequent challenges or crises. For our work in personal leadership development, we will focus on Erikson's stages that happen in adulthood. We need to highlight that he proposes some indicative age brackets, but we understand that as we live longer those may not always represent what we see today. These stages also comprise long periods of time, even decades, so they are far more complex than the summary below. Erikson's developmental stages in adulthood, and how these might be translated into career decisions, are summarised as:

Early Adulthood (basic conflict: intimacy vs. isolation): According to Erikson, this stage occurs around the ages of 19–29 years, although we do not think an age band is necessarily important. The primary task is to establish intimate, meaningful relationships with others. Trust and commitment with others are an important factor so we can establish bonds beyond our family of origin. It is easier to see examples of this stage of development in our personal lives, as we commit to romantic relationships and form friendships. However, our career decisions can be also influenced by this developmental stage's focus on intimacy and isolation. When professional choices are aligned with one's innermost desires and values, they are informed by intimacy. The other extreme is when individuals make decisions informed by isolation, and choose to conform to external expectations or follow a path they dislike primarily for those reasons. The level of fulfilment, alignment with passion, and the depth of connections formed in one's career can greatly influence the experience of intimacy or isolation in this context. Intimacy requires a level of openness to be vulnerable as it links to a deeper need for connection. Successful resolution leads to the ability to form deep connections and experience genuine intimacy; in terms of career it may mean being able to reconcile passion and meaning with practical aspects, such as financial gains or social desirability.

Mid-adulthood (basic conflict: generativity vs. stagnation): According to Erikson, this stage spans across a large proportion of adulthood, between the ages of 30–64 years. This tends to be the stage we talk about when delivering personal leadership development workshops and it centres around contributing to society and future generations. This process involves finding purpose in work, parenthood, and other activities and building a positive legacy from living according to our values and passions. At work, this means making a positive impact that goes beyond self, which could be through mentoring or simply by creating a culture that is positive and enables others to develop and thrive. Many of us experience this, especially as we achieve more senior positions, and we may find ourselves gradually turning our focus to caring for our team, organisation or even society regardless of any immediate personal gains. Stagnation is related to playing safe, not risking being disappointed by pursuing our aspirations or investing in others. This is a real paradox because as we avoid risk, we also avoid realising ourselves. Stagnation often brings a sense of regret or missed opportunity, of being trapped in a meaningless and unfulfilling life. On the other hand, the sense of purpose and agency that accompanies generativity often brings a feeling of personal fulfilment.

Late Adulthood (basic conflict: integrity vs. despair): Erikson indicates that this stage emerges from the age 65. We need to be mindful that we now live much longer lives and in practice, this stage may start quite a bit later. At this point, individuals reflect on their lives and evaluate their accomplishments. Reflections on the meaning of one's life become evident and understanding what life was all about is an important aspect. A sense of integrity is achieved by accepting the life one has lived, finding meaning in past experiences, and embracing wisdom. Despair arises from a sense of regret, unfulfilled goals, or a fear of death. Like the other stages in Erikson, here there is a theme of daring to be ourselves and of living purposefully or trying to avoid disappointment and rejection. It is important to point out that when we are pursuing meaningful activities and relationships, we are making ourselves vulnerable; and at times we need to accept failure or rejection as part of our learning process. So, it is not all rosy, and it will definitely not look the same for everyone.

Both Jung and Erikson highlight the importance of achieving a sense of identity, establishing meaningful relationships, making productive contributions, and finding fulfilment in later life. They emphasise how personal development continues throughout adulthood, and how what we pursue in different stages of life will change with time. There is no ending point to this process, and a longer life opens up the possibilities for self-exploration and growth. Of course, we also see people stuck with unresolved issues and conflicts, bringing some of them with them from earlier stages of life. Likewise, we see many people in our own workshops gaining awareness of these unresolved issues, and finally committing to resolve them. The task is never easy, but it can be surprisingly rewarding to discover who we really are. When we invest in our personal leadership, going through different psychosocial stages and entering the second half of life, we are well positioned to develop a sense of wholeness, wisdom, and a deepened understanding of oneself and others.

2.3 The development of mind

Another key adult development author informing our model is Robert Kegan (1982; 1995). Similar to Erikson, he builds on the work of pioneers in psychology to explore the development of self through the life span. Inspired by Jean Piaget's research on child development, Kegan explores how we, as adults, make sense of our thoughts and feelings and relationships with others and with ourselves. In his constructive development theory, Kegan argues that as we grow and develop, we construct different frames to see the world. We are also able to identify, unpack and challenge frames we use to continue developing ourselves. This ability to develop our thinking in adulthood has been linked to the notion of neuroplasticity of the brain from neuroscience, and the fact that, contrary to what was previously believed, we continue developing cognitively into old age.

Drawing from Kegan's work we would like to focus on the three qualitatively different stages of development that happen during adulthood. The first refers to the transition from adolescence to early adulthood. At this stage our needs are no longer the sole focus of our concern. Instead, we start taking into consideration what our social groups need or expect from us. For example, this is the stage when a young person will start doing or not doing something, not because of the consequences to themselves, but because of how their actions will impact others. For example, a teenager will tidy up their room not because they would not be allowed on their mobile phones otherwise, but because they know it would help their parents. Kegan calls this stage the socialised mind because we become more part of society and society becomes more part of us. This means that at this stage, we're looking to live more aligned with our contexts in terms of values and norms in expectations, and that becomes an important part of how we approach decisions and experiences.

While this is a good thing, as it means we are now in a position of living up to the expectations of society, as responsible and trustworthy citizens, this is only the first stage of adult development. This is because life in society is a bit more complex than that, and it's important that adults are in a position to step back from all these expectations, in order to make up their own minds on what is right or wrong. A good example of that is things that we find unacceptable today that in the past were deemed completely fine. We are sure all of us have a couple of examples we could share. For instance, when many of us were children, it was not unacceptable for a teacher to smoke in a classroom, or a doctor to smoke in their practice as they see patients. This works both ways; some things that were not acceptable in the past have been normalised, like using a mobile phone during mealtimes. We will stay away from expressing a judgment on this habit – but just to point out that this is not uncommon and not necessarily seen as unacceptable. So, the point here is that if all of us stayed in our basic level of 'socialised' development, no one would be challenging the status quo and the norms that may actually improve society as a whole. Of course, we also see changes that may not be all so positive, such as the mobile phone example, but the point is that without this level of development no one would be questioning the system. As our society and lives become more individualised and we are presented with a greater variety of choice, the socialised mind is too simplistic to effectively process the world out there. This will take us to the next stage of development which is called the self-authoring mind. At this stage we are able to develop the ability to make more complex decisions independently.

At the self-authoring stage, we develop an internal judgement, and the personal authority to evaluate the world and our experiences independently of what society expects from us. This is the point when we start becoming our own person, authoring our own identity. For example, a project manager who is in the self-authoring stage of development may run a project not only following the set guidelines, but building on their expertise to identify and solve issues, or to make improvements, that have not been anticipated in the guidelines. Therefore, they are looking beyond the information given. Self-authoring individuals are much more comfortable with embracing changes (including technological changes) or in taking a coaching approach to management rather than an authoritative one. This is because they are comfortable exploring the world beyond the obvious boundaries of the status quo. According to Kegan, most adults would stay within these two stages (socialised or self-authoring mind) over the course of their adult lives, with the majority reaching only the socialised mind.

A small number of individuals continue to develop to the final stage described by Kegan, called the self-transforming mind. In this level of consciousness, individuals comfortably engage with complexity, ambiguity and opposing ideologies without being attached to roles, identities, and any preconceived ideas of how they should behave. Therefore, self-transformers are prepared to let go of control and the sense of security of having right and wrong answers. Kegan describes them as the true self-actualisers as they continuously adapt, shift and update their mental models in response to new learnings.

It is important to note that between each of these stages of consciousness there is a long period of transition and development. Finally, Kegan makes an explicit connection between these levels of consciousness and longevity. As learning opportunities and challenges are essential to move us out of our comfort zone and expand our level of consciousness, and the longer we live the more opportunities we are likely to have to be challenged to progress in our development. For the purpose of our sustainable personal leadership model, it is not our developmental stage that matters, but the principle that we have the potential to continue growing and improving. Thus, when we achieve qualitative better ways of seeing the world, we can also unlock new and better ways of experiencing life.

2.4 Identity construction

Our self-concept, or identity, is an important aspect to understanding ourselves and our career development. This has been evident in the theories we described here. Thus, we also draw on identity research to understand how we develop and redevelop our self-concept. This is a vast area of study with many important scholars and researchers. Some key authors include Herminia Ibarra (see 2003; 2007; 2023), Blake Ashforth (see 2001) and Andrew Brown (see 2015). The research is quite fragmented, so we will broadly summarise some of the key aspects.

The concept of identity answers the question 'who am I?' Identity can be defined as the various meanings attached to someone either by themselves or by others; these meanings may derive from social roles, group affiliations, traits and/or personality. This means that there are several aspects of our lives that will at any given time contribute to our overall self-concept. Although we often talk about our identity as one object, we do, in fact, have several identities in relation to different aspects of our lives. For example: Both of us (Kelly and Tatiana) are academics, so our work identity links to that occupation. At the same time, our academic areas are different, which will influence the meaning of being an academic to each of us. The same applies to other identities, as a parent, a daughter or as a friend. Each of these meanings, sub-identities, contributes to our sense of self.

Although we have these multiple sub-identities, the way we make sense of them may vary depending on the centrality or importance of each specific identity to us. For instance, when someone is studying at university the identity as student is foregrounded and may be central to most of their activities and decisions. When this person graduates and joins the world of work, this may be replaced by a work identity. If they eventually return to higher education, for an MBA for instance, they may have these two identities active, but not necessarily carrying the same weight. If, for example, the work identity is more central and suddenly the person is faced with competing demands, they would be more likely to drop or pause the student identity without necessarily feeling they are challenging who they are.

In the same way that we can hold several sub-identities, our identities are continuously being shaped by our circumstances and life events. For example, when someone is promoted, as they move from being a team member to be the team leader, they will inevitably experience an identity transition linked to a change in role. We could say that to take this leadership position, the person is pushed to make adjustments to their identity. Another example is when someone retires from a particular career that plays a central role in who they are, e.g., a retiring sportsperson, they will need to seek other identities to fill the void. More likely, they will need to find a renewed work identity. This may be similar to the previous one, e.g., sports coach, or completely different, e.g., an accountant, depending how much the identity lost is central to the individual. So, although we talk about our sense of self as if it were a stable notion, the reality is that we are constantly adjusting and adapting who we are in light of our experiences and relationships. While this may seem to take away any certainty of who we are, it is important to remember that identity construction and transitions are an important part of adult development and ageing well. We do not simply overwrite our previous identity with new ones. Instead, the way in which we evolve and construct our identities gets captured in our personal narrative (see Chapters 4, 5), the story of our journey, connecting the thread of our past, present and future in a coherent way.

The process of constructing an identity involves experimenting with different possible selves before we can commit to it. For instance, when someone moves abroad as an expatriate, that identity starts to be developed in the first host country. One can, in effect, 'decide' what kind of person they will be in this new context. So, what kind of clique one will join, what will be the routines, activities and hobbies. Even once you've adopted this new identity, you can move on and reshape this identity further in a following host country. This process can be quite playful, imaginative and exploratory, or more committed and systematic if we are under greater pressure to define it. Either way, it is not an easy task and involves a lot of experimentation and reflection. These two processes are an integral part of our sustainable personal leadership model.

2.5 The bottom line

The theories we have briefly introduced in this previous section inform several important aspects of our sustainable personal leadership model. Our aim is not to exhaust them here but to pinpoint where some of our insights come from conceptually and how these connect with our experience of working with midlife professionals and executives on their personal leadership development. We will be applying these ideas when discussing each element of our model and the ways we can apply them to practice. Before we continue, however, we think it is important to highlight the key takeaways.

When it comes to careers and our working lives, the person (self) is the most important factor. Our career outcomes tend to be more positive when they are informed by our values, desires and developmental needs. This includes feeling more fulfilled and in an environment that is aligned with us. The person is the driver of their own career development in the new world of work. Although some organisations still plan their employees' talent development, the onus of managing one's career and evaluating the next move or decision lies with individuals. So, the person is central to leading their career outcomes.

Adulthood includes several phases and stages of development, each with its own set of priorities, desires and aspirations that will emerge and fade over time. Different opportunities to learn will appear that will allow us to gain perspective and insight. We may also be faced with changed needs. Either way, one way of living will not serve us well throughout. So, adjustment and adaptability are key. Finally, as we navigate different experiences, roles and relationships, we are required to shape who we are. Our identity and sense of self is always evolving. While this 'work in progress' status of our self-concept can, sometimes, be demanding and emotionally challenging, it opens fantastic opportunities to experience life in many, different ways. In the new era of increased longevity, this is more exciting than ever.

Chapter 3
Longevity, work and retirement

In the previous chapter we explored some of the important research in the fields of career, adult development, and identity construction that we draw on in developing our thinking. In this chapter, we will look at the demographic realities brought about by increased longevity. We will reflect on the history of 'retirement' and how social and demographic pressures are changing how we think about retirement. We will conclude with some discussion about the role of personal development and lifelong learning in ensuring that work and careers can fit with our longer lives.

3.1 Changing global demographics

We cannot start exploring sustainable personal leadership development without first exploring the context of this conversation. The main aspect we have to highlight is the dramatic ageing of the global population that has been observed by gerontologists, sociologists, economists, and human geographers in the past few decades. Population ageing has also been a subject in the agenda of governments, policymakers and international organisations, such as the World Health Organisation (WHO), the Organisation for Economic Co-operation and Development (OECD), the United Nations (UN) and the International Labour Office (ILO) – and discussions have intensified in the past few years. The topic has also reached wider audiences through books (e.g., *The 100-year Life* by Lynda Gratton and Andrew Scott; *The SuperAge* by Bradley Schurman) and the work of charities and age diverse campaign groups (e.g., The International Longevity Centre; the Centre for Ageing Better, the American Association of Retired Persons [AARP]). Despite the increased awareness of the potential impact of an ageing population, there has been little action from industry and businesses.

Tatiana, who often gives talks on the subject of ageing well and work, has noticed that in the past couple of years this topic has started to attract the interest of business leaders and working people. At large, participants seem motivated to think about how *they* (personally) will approach their midlife transitions and late career. This is a positive sign, especially because until now people shied away from the subject unless they were at the verge of retirement. Because of this lack of interest in the subject until recently, there has been very little change in how we think about and approach our lives, work, career and retirement since the mid-20th century. Consequently, the way work is designed has not adapted to changes in population. Even after the COVID-19 pandemic, which in many ways disrupted how we work, we do not see any major innovation on work design that may be more aligned with population trends. Figure 3.1 gives an overall picture of how the global demographic composition has changed.

https://doi.org/10.1515/9783111316147-003

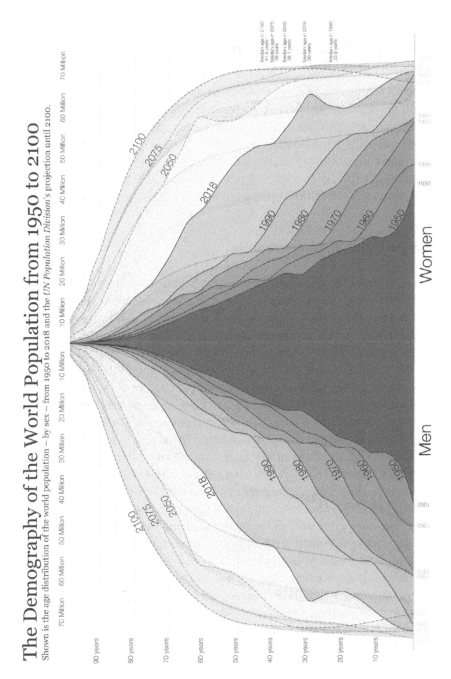

Figure 3.1: World population 1950 to 2100.
Source: The United Nations Population Division – World Population Prospects 2017; Medium Variant. The data visualization is available at OurWorldinData.org, where you can find more research on how the world is changing and why. Licensed under CC-BY by the author Max Roser.

The trend towards ageing of the population started steadily from the 19th century as societies became more industrialised and living conditions improved, e.g., access to medical care, sanitation, vaccination programmes. The WHO (2002) called this ageing phenomena a triumph in addressing premature mortality and disease, which in turn has increased global longevity. The projections shown in Figure 3.1 may have slightly changed since this visualisation was produced, however, the expected change in the shape of the population distribution from a 'pyramid' to a 'pillar' is still valid at a global level. According to analysis from the UN) (2022) population age distribution varies significantly between countries. Nevertheless, population ageing is a prevailing global trend driven by the demographic transition, which involves longer lifespans and smaller family sizes, even in countries with relatively youthful populations. An older population is already a reality in many regions, for example Europe and Northern America which combined have the highest concentration of older persons. Other parts of the globe, for instance Northern Africa, Western Asia, and sub-Saharan Africa, are anticipated to observe a rapid expansion in the number of older individuals over the next three decades. This means those countries that are just starting to face this change in the profile of the population will be under greater pressure to adapt.

If we look at Figure 3.1, within the next century we will be reaching a tipping point where the number of older individuals is expected to exceed the number of young children. The UN (2023) estimates that, globally, the number of individuals aged 65 years or above is likely to more than double, increasing from 761 million in 2021 to 1.6 billion by 2050. This means that while in 2021, one out of every ten individuals globally was aged 65 or older, by 2050, one in six individuals worldwide will be over the age of 65 years. Women typically outnumber men at older ages, but the gap in longevity will likely decrease (see UN 2022; 2023).

Lower fertility level (birth rate) is one of the factors leading to population ageing. According to the UN (2022), approximately two thirds of the world's population live in an area or country where there are fewer than 2.1 births per woman, a fertility level that equates to zero growth over time when low mortality is assumed. For example: Across the OECD, fertility rates have fallen from 3.45 births per woman in 1960 to 1.58 in 2020. As birth rates decrease, the proportion of younger people diminishes, leading to a rise in the percentages of working-age adults and, subsequently, older adults. This means not only that the age profile of the population will increase, but that the size of the population will also drop over time as fewer babies are born. Some countries will experience significant reductions in population size by 2050, for example Bulgaria, Japan, Latvia, Lithuania, Serbia, and Ukraine, due to low birth rates as well as emigration (UN, 2022).

Global mobility and migration add complexity to population changes, indicating that this issue is more than a simple equation of births vs. deaths. High-income countries have seen more population growth from migration than from births and deaths, while low-income and lower-middle-income countries continue to experience population growth primarily due to birth rates. Some countries have seen substantial immigration due to refugee movements, while others have experienced net emigration driven by labour movements, insecurity, and conflict.

Migration can relieve some of the issues of an ageing workforce in developed countries by increasing the number of people of working age in the population. Nevertheless, this is not a future-proof solution to be relied upon given that ageing is a trend observed in most countries. This is like moving from one pocket to another – the human resources overall remain the same. Or worse, lower income countries end up facing issues of brain drain and gaps of qualified workers that make their own social-economic situation even more challenging. An alternative, and more sustainable, solution to increase the pool of workers is to grow the numbers of older workers. This means creating the conditions that incentivise extending one's career through delaying retirement. This approach is more aligned with the realities of population changes.

This is supported by an analysis of social-economic implications of the population ageing, which can be demonstrated by the increase in the old-age dependency ratio. This ratio is defined as the number of individuals aged 65 and over per 100 people of working age (20–64 years old) and it is often used as an approximation of economic dependency. In OECD countries, the old age demographic ratio was 22.5% in 2000, 33.1% in 2023 and is predicted to be 58.6% in 2075 – if the current parameters of retirement and exit of the labour force remain unchanged. Within the age-dependency ratio scenario just described, increasingly, older workers will be pushed to delay their retirement. This adds to the argument for longer working lives, and further reinforces the strategic imperative to retain older individuals in the workforce to ensure robust manpower to keep the economy functioning.

Population ageing often has been framed as a social problem, but this is only part of the story. The potential of encouraging greater labour force participation of individuals aged 50 and over is immense. This can be illustrated by some figures from the AARP, OECD and World Economic Forum Living, Learning, and Earning Longer Learning Collaborative initiative. According to their report, merely increasing the employment levels of workers aged 50 across OECD countries in line with the countries with the highest participation of 50+ workers, can potentially increase GDP across OECD nations by a staggering $10.3 trillion. This economic boost effectively counteracts the potential loss incurred if the employment rates of older workers stagnate, underscoring the significance of their active participation (see AARP, 2020).

The opportunities go beyond supplying additional human resources in the economy. Older individuals are potential consumers, carers and able to add immense value to society. However, new realities demand new ways of being, and so a different approach to life and work. Just over 20 years ago WHO (2002) launched its active ageing campaign, aiming to encourage healthy living and active participation of older individuals within an age-friendly society. This approach to longevity is not simply a set of target actions for older people. Of course, these are needed, but these need to be combined with societal actions to ensure active ageing for generations to come. Hence, the importance of educating younger and midlife individuals to think ahead and prepare themselves by monitoring their health, social and economic participation.

Active ageing is still high in the WHO's policy agenda and together with the UN they launched a new campaign in 2022 named 'a world for all ages'. This campaign acknowledges the importance of an effective multigenerational society where all age groups can thrive. One of their key targets is to tackle ageism that prevents people of all ages from fully participating. These campaigns are important and positive steps, but unless more of us start taking action 'on the ground' the change will be very slow. As individuals, professionals, and leaders in our fields, it is our responsibility to be part of this paradigm shift. If not for the good of future generations, which is an honourable cause to care about, we must act for our own benefit, to secure the kind of opportunities we would like to have in the future. It is important that we have skin in the game when it comes to the longevity economy and it is not all rhetoric.

3.2 The invention of retirement

The relationship between people and work reflects labour force and societal needs, demands and opportunities. As socio-economic context changes, this relationship evolves and changes. Over the course of history, we can see that this is not only true for older workers, but also for women and 'underage' workers. So, it is not a surprise that given the demographics shift and other developments (e.g., technological advancements), we are starting to see a shift in late working life and retirement attitudes and behaviours. Retirement is a relatively recent social phenomenon, gaining significant prominence during the latter half of the 20th century. This view is supported by various scholars in the field of age and employment (see Atchley, 2000; Graebner, 1980; Künemund & Kolland, 2007; Phillipson, 1990; Phillipson & Smith, 2005). In medieval times, for example, people worked as long as they could, driven by the absence of a pension system to replace work income. As the industrial revolution developed, the need to renew the workforce, by replacing older workers with younger ones, contributed to the creation of the institution of retirement as a legitimate way to withdraw from work and still retain a modest amount of income. In effect, the development of retirement as a distinct life stage is largely due to social security systems that provide income for older people, enabling them to leave the workforce.

Retirement as a social and economic institution expanded steadily between the 1950s and late 1960s. During this time financial provision in retirement became institutionalised and, in many countries, occupational pensions became more common. As a result, retirement was increasingly seen as a legitimate stage of life, accepted and expected by many workers. The period from the late 1960s to the 1980s brought significant changes, marked by high unemployment levels and increased flexibility to work patterns. Early retirement policies were introduced among the strategies used to control the effects of unemployment in many contexts. In Europe, for instance, early retirement appeared to have become a mass phenomenon by the early 1970s and 1980s, and led to an increase in the number of years individuals would be in retirement.

By early to mid-2000s, the trend of early retirement was showing signs of reversing. This was partially fuelled by extending working life policies and the removal of a mandatory retirement age in many countries. Reversing early retirement behaviours was an important and positive development given that increased longevity already extended the number of years in retirement. The COVID-19 pandemic may have disrupted this trend. It is too early to ascertain the long-term impact, especially at a global level. Emerging evidence indicates, however, that many older workers decided to retire early during the pandemic and some are now trying to 'unretire'.

Alongside these different socio-economic influences on the timing of retirement, midlife experiences started to become more varied; thus, people of the same age may be at completely different stages of life. For example, while one person may be envisaging retirement and downsizing of their family home, another of the same age group may be just starting a family and would have completely different needs. Both scenarios are considered socially acceptable and it shows that people now may approach their mid and late career in different ways. The transition to retirement, therefore, has shifted from a standardised process to an individualised one. Thus, the idea of retirement has become more nuanced, meaning different things for people which has an impact in how each of us think about our late career and end of working life.

The term 'retirement' itself is ambiguous because it can refer to an event, a process, a status, a role or a phase of life, and it can have its meaning attached to different objective and subjective criteria, such as work, income, pension receipt, career changes, as well as individuals' subjective self-assessment. Therefore, conversations around retirement can be related to distinct issues. As we write here about retirement, we are very aware that this topic resonates differently with our readers depending on how we think about it. This is not different from what we see in our workshops; some participants strongly reject these conversations, while others are quite open to understanding why we are talking about an issue that they may still feel fairly removed from. Our main point is that while retirement is perceived by many as a separate stage in the life of a worker, following a period of paid employment or self-employment, in reality this later stage is closely connected to one's working life. Therefore, it cannot be an afterthought. What happens at the end of our career is very much a consequence of the advantages and disadvantages we accumulated over the course of our lives. This being especially the case when we look at the relationship between midlife experiences and late-life outcomes.

Retirement no longer means *the end*; the individualisation of career trajectories shows that there are many versions of retirement. More often than not, retirement includes work. While work in late life is often unpaid (e.g., volunteering, caring), remunerated work is also observed in late life. This is why we see terms like 'encore career', 'fuller working lives', 'phased retirement' as attempts to capture the different variations. We call it 'engaged retirement' to emphasise activities, whether it is paid, unpaid work or leisure, that is meaningful to us. Because, according to theorists in adult development (see Chapter 2), 'meaning' becomes increasingly important from midlife onwards. Therefore, this later career stage, whatever name you decide to adopt, offers opportunities for continuity, or even development of new identities.

For engaged retirement to happen, however, we need to be open and prepared to seize opportunities as they are presented to us. Being prepared is at the heart of it. For us to make the most of our increased longevity it is necessary to be a step ahead. Of course, some people are lucky. We accept that happens, but evidence is quite clear that individuals who think about short- as well as long-term gains or consequences tend to fare better. Thus, retirement and late-life conversations should always be on the agenda. This is the 'sustainable' aspect of personal leadership and it should inform how we navigate our careers and development.

3.3 Careers across time

Let's reflect together on how work and careers have changed over the generations. Inspired by the work of Max Weber (see Swedberg, 2018), we will use some examples as ideal types or a typical person as a frame of reference. The word 'ideal' here is a technical term to indicate we are not referring to a specific person, and does not mean perfect or desirable. We acknowledge that there are always exceptional cases and variations, as well as national or regional differences to the ideal types we will use. With that caveat in mind, let's start with Julius as a typical worker in our grand-fathers' generation. We expect that Julius probably worked his whole life on the same kind of job, probably at the same company. So, if Julius was a salesman, he may have retired a sales manager, or a senior salesman. If he was an engineer, we expect a similar pattern. We would also expect that at some point, probably in his late 50s or early 60s he would be retiring. So, a linear career pattern: education – work – retirement.

Now let's move to our parents' generation. We will name the typical worker Carl and will assume the same caveats of possible variations or exceptions. We can expect that Carl would have worked all his life in the same line of work, and probably would have worked for more than one company doing a similar job. So, if Carl was a salesman in company X, he could have moved to company Y to become the sales manager. But Carl world have a few contemporaries that would have been a bit more daring, who would perhaps have moved to careers that drew on the similar skills and knowledge base, for example from engineering to finance. In most cases the career trajectory observed is also simple: education – work (including some transitions) – retirement. Patterns of retirement would also have occurred around the same age as Julius, if not a bit earlier.

As the reader may have noticed, both our previous examples are male workers; sadly, despite any exceptions we may find, broadly speaking the career patterns for women in previous generations were not stable enough to make them a typical worker. So, to get a bit more gender balance in our next example we will refer to Mary as the typical worker of our generation. The catch is that typical is starting to vary a lot more now. For example, Mary started her career in sales. Having discovered a passion for marketing, she decided to complete a marketing qualification which allowed her to formally move into a marketing function. She changed jobs a couple of times. With her last employer, Mary was also involved in commercial and strategy aspects which allowed her to learn more about corporate strategy on the job. At some point in her early 50s, Mary decided to quit her corporate career and set up a small strategic marketing consultancy where she can use her knowledge and skills in a variety of companies that would not have this function in-house. Mary's plan is that in a few years she will start cutting down her hours, but as she still enjoys her work, full retirement is still not in the cards.

Over the course of her career, Mary could have made all sorts of other changes, such as moving countries, retraining again, taking a maternity break, etc. This is because careers trajectories can be a lot more varied as well as influenced by other life domains. This means that the working life of a typical person today is significantly more complex and more prone to change due to external factors, such as job market shifts, as well as internal factors such as identity transitions or personal circumstances. Thus, a career trajectory between the initial education and retirement for our generation may include twists and turns, retraining, part-time work, breaks, retirement and unretirement.

The main point we would like to emphasise is that careers are increasingly varied and changeable now. This is a shift from the predictable and linear career paths of our parents and grandparents' generations. While there are plenty of explanations for this phenomenon, such as weakened social contracts between employers and employees, generational differences, changing aspirations and consumption patterns, longevity is also an important factor in the individualisation and flexibility of career trajectories. Successfully managing the potential of longer lives requires adaptability and frequent adjustments to our lifestyle. This is not only because we need to change things to match our overall fitness, health, and energy levels, but we also feel compelled to make changes in our work or personal lives so these can provide new life experiences or opportunities for learning. So, simply elongating Julius' or Carl's career pattern would not work today, because even though we are healthier than ever before, the clock does not stop. We still age and mature and, therefore, will not want the same things in our 50s or 60s as we wanted in our 30s. It is safe to say in the era of increased longevity, extended career trajectories are not necessarily the maintenance of 'sameness' for longer. Instead, these involve embracing other, different experiences that can bring greater fulfilment. This is important because there is a financial pressure to continue working for longer, but this should not inevitably be on the same terms or doing the same things as in earlier stages of life.

Extended career trajectories must be sustainable, this means that work should be compatible with individuals' personal circumstances. In the future, we should be able to see more people like Mary, who is able to make choices and changes that work for her. This includes career reinventions, phased retirement, reduced working hours or an encore career. For that to be possible, we need a combination of individual readiness and societal acceptance. At the individual level, this means being prepared to make adjustments and changes well ahead of reaching late career. As we have already highlighted, it is as early as midlife that preparation starts. Because by the time we get close to retirement age, if you are not prepared or the conditions are not favourable, the range of options available is a lot more limited. The aim here is not a one-size-fits-all solution, but to have greater choice and control over what happens to us. What we choose as a result is personal and somewhat less important. Being prepared requires a conscious effort, and a commitment to develop our personal leadership. How to do this is very much central to the topic of this book.

3.4 Cyclical careers

At a societal level, we need to change our norms and expectations around work and career, so we can create more opportunities for individualised trajectories (instead of one-size-fits-all). Back in the 1980s, the sociologist Fred Best had already proposed a loosening of what he called the education-work-retirement lockstep model. He argued that this linear, and to a certain extent rigid, life course pattern needs to be replaced by a more flexible model. Best called for a cyclical approach which enables individuals to move in and out of different types of educational, work and leisure activities over the course of their lives. We can confidently say that the world has changed considerably since the 1980s, however, this cyclical approach has not yet fully materialised. We would dare to suggest that, on balance, we are closer to the linear model than the flexible one. While many people manage to return to education and redirect their careers, often quite successfully, very few manage a career sabbatical that is not frowned upon. An example is how women, who have taken time off for raising their children, face a penalty for this decision when returning to work.

Most of us are complicit with this linear life course pattern, even if we are not aware of it. It is not uncommon to hear comments like: 'How strange to receive this job application from someone who could be doing a better paid job elsewhere, there must be something wrong with them'; 'This person's CV shows that they took this long work leave, how odd is that? Would they leave us suddenly too? Or are they not committed to their work?' It does take a conscious effort not to negatively judge a CV that has long gaps, or a job application from someone changing direction. This is because by default we assess these situations based on social norms and expectations that reflect this linear life course. We make these evaluations without even being aware that we are complying with these dated norms and expectations. Those idealised standards, however, no longer fit the needs and realities of individuals today or in the future. This is because living longer lives in the context of today's society leads to significantly more complex and individualised career trajectories.

The case for flexible or cyclical career patterns is clearer than ever. In addition to more openness to unusual career trajectories and choices, there are another three important aspects this new approach to working lives needs. To some extent, these have been highlighted by De Vos and colleagues (2020) when arguing for sustainable careers (see also Tomlinson et al., 2018). The first is that work arrangements need to take into consideration our age-related adjustments. For example, changing interests and aspirations, or levels of fitness and health. We are not implying we will be sick as we age, although many do live with chronic conditions. Instead, our working lives should allow us to remain in good health and for that they should offer flexibility in work arrangements. We often see this in sports, when athletes move on from certain competitive categories or from the sport altogether because it is time they give their bodies a rest. This, however, is not very common in other occupations.

The second aspect is work that offers opportunities for lifelong learning. In October 2023, Tatiana attended a closed workshop organised by the OECD and AARP and the main message was that lifelong learning is the 21st century's job security. In fact, the case for learning and development is strongly supported by evidence from studies on late career employability. For example, evidence says that long-tenure workers, whose jobs tend to be fairly unchanged over the years, are the ones who tend to be worse off in terms of skills and knowledge that make them employable. Learning enables us to become adaptable and responsive to change. Lifelong learning not only helps us to update our knowledge and skills but also improves our ability to learn new things at a faster pace. Thus, it improves our thinking and our ability to solve problems. Learning, however, should not be reduced to going back to the classroom or education. Even though we see the powerful effects of formal learning when working with MBA students, learning can be drawn from less formalised experiences if we are open to different perspectives. When we are forced to adapt, change or are exposed to new working practices, culture or thinking, we also learn. This is often reported by professionals who are assigned to work abroad or move job functions. In addition to contributing to greater employability, lifelong learning also enables us to discover new areas of interest, hidden talents that we would not be aware of unless by moving out of business as usual.

The third aspect is life management strategies. Longer lives and careers require us to embrace the individualised nature of adulthood and create the conditions and the skills for life management strategies. For that, we need to develop an understanding of the factors that contribute to positive or negative outcomes in later life and how individuals and context can influence those. In practice, this means recognising how advantages and disadvantages (e.g., money, time, social support, good or bad health) accumulate and interact so we can make choices that optimise or preserve our resources for longer. Thus, through greater self-awareness, self-knowledge and personal leadership we learn how to manage ourselves in a way that we can maximise our level of choice and control later in life. Organisations and societies also need to create the conditions, e.g., through flexibility, support and opportunities, to allow individuals to exercise life management strategies that underpin a sustainable career.

3.5 The bottom line

In this chapter, we examined the demographic changes in ageing and population that have resulted in increased longevity. We looked at the relatively short history of retirement and how the notions of retirement that most 'midlifers' will have been raised to expect are rapidly changing. We have built the social and economic case for longer working lives and engaged retirement. We have also discussed how career patterns changed over time. We argued the case for cyclical instead of linear career patterns.

The result is that late career is being reinvented. Some individuals may continue working, others may retrain and embark on a second or third career, while still others may be exiting the paid workforce altogether. In every case, this will be an individualised picture; there is no longer any one-size-fits-all model.

Chapter 4
The new midlife

In the previous chapter we explored the demographic and socio-economic developments that are informing how we should be thinking about our careers and working lives. We explored how we are in the middle of this change in paradigm and how we are inevitably shaping what this extra longevity means for the next generations. This chapter will continue this discussion by exploring midlife as a stage of life. We will explain how at this point in our trajectories we have enough experience to know what works and what doesn't work for us. We will also explore how this awareness about ourselves and our contexts can be valuable in shaping our midlife and future experiences. More importantly, how personal leadership gives us agency to change what happens next.

4.1 Life course and lifespan: two theories

When exploring the adult, careers, and personal leadership development literature, it is inevitable that we will come across a variety of terminologies to frame how events and factors influence our development over our lifetime. The temptation is to use terms such as life stages, lifespan or life course interchangeably; however, technically speaking, these are attached to particular perspectives on human development. Despite the great overlap between these perspectives, they are conceptualised around different assumptions and applications. We think it is useful to examine these distinctions and how the contribution from each field of research can help us to understand better the dynamics of sustainable personal leadership. We will build on a recent paper by Zacher and Froidevaux (2021) in which they discuss how these concepts have been used in career research.

Life stages models frame life and career as a series of discrete, normative and age-bound stages with associated developmental tasks which when completed, allow the person to progress to a next stage linearly. An example of that is Erik Erikson's psychosocial development theory we described in Chapter 2. Most of the ideas developed within the life stages' perspective are still valid today but the way we use them has changed slightly. In particular, instead of assuming that development happens in discrete stages, most models now view development as a continuous and more malleable process.

Lifespan approach, however, entails a bit more than a new perspective to life stages models and theories. Originating from developmental psychology research, it posits that individual development is a lifelong, continuous and multidirectional endeavour. Moreover, its process and outcomes are influenced by an interplay of biological, contextual and regulatory factors. Therefore, lifespan approaches accept that

https://doi.org/10.1515/9783111316147-004

human development is not only influenced by the individuals themselves, but also their environment and their responses. For example, lifespan studies allowed us to understand that fluid and crystalised intelligence changes with age; contrary to the popular belief, it is not all downhill. Quite the opposite: There is now evidence that we continue to develop our crystalised intelligence until very late life (see Cattell, 1971; Horn, 1989; Tucker-Drob et al., 2019). Lifespan research also explores how our approaches to problem solving change with age and how we tend to prioritise positive emotional experiences and meaningful social connections as we get older (Carstensen, 2006; Charles & Carstensen, 2010). Finally, one of the greatest contributions of the lifespan perspective is to bring several areas of knowledge together to help us to understand how we can thrive at any age. With respect to ageing well, there are several regulatory processes that contribute to how one can age well and achieve what some would call successful ageing.

While lifespan studies have remained within the domain of psychology, a relatively similar approach has emerged in the field of sociology. The life course perspective also takes a longitudinal view on individual development. However, instead of emphasising individual aspects, life course has focused on contextual factors that may influence one's biography and overall trajectory. These contextual aspects include societal systems, structures, institutions, and historical moments, for example social class, schooling, family composition, cultural norms and expectations, etc. Prior life histories, including the experiences of parents and grandparents, as well as interpersonal relationships (i.e., linked-lives concept), may influence one's trajectory. For example, your university experience is likely to be shaped by your parents' experiences if, for instance, you are the first in the family to go to higher education. A similar example would be career decisions which may be influenced by our partners' career/ life decisions or an unexpected caring responsibility. Broadly speaking, life course theories often explore the relationship between social structures and agency, individuals' ability to take action and drive their own agenda in a given set of conditions. Within this context, life course looks at how our life trajectories (and outcomes) are affected by our experience of transitions and the advantages and disadvantages we accumulate throughout our lives.

Although these different strands of research emphasise different processes, they are not necessarily conflicting. In fact, there is much to gain from considering both individual and contextual aspects in tandem and many emerging theories in career and personal development are looking to integrate them. An example is the concept of career sustainability that we introduced in Chapter 2. The main insight these approaches to development bring is the idea that development is a continuum and there is little point in looking at different life stages in isolation. This may sound obvious, but this view was not always taken by scholars researching adult development and ageing. So, at whatever stage of life we are, we are always a product of our past. This is not to say we must be trapped by this past; quite the contrary, understanding internal and external influences in our lives gives us choice. It allows us to achieve the self-authoring stage Kegan talks about – thus, it enables us to examine ourselves and our context critically and be in a position to make conscious decisions on how we want to proceed. This ability to reflect on our lives allows us to free ourselves from blindly abiding by the expectations and norms imposed on us. For example, it helps us to redirect our career once we understand what matters to us personally or let go of limiting beliefs and unhelpful labels we carry with us. This choice, whether we call it self-authoring, or self-efficacy or simply agency, is ultimately what personal leadership is all about.

The acknowledgement of a life trajectory, which connects past experiences and influencing factors to our present and future has led researchers to recognise the significance of key life events and transitions in shaping individual development over time. While some transitions are unique to some individuals – for instance not everyone will have children, get married or get divorced – other transitions such as adolescence and midlife are expected of most of us. These transitional periods became more relevant as society changed and we started to live longer. While adolescence is a very interesting and rich area of research, most of the topics we are exploring in this book are very much situated in the context of midlife. This does not mean that the points we are raising are not relevant to individuals who do not consider themselves in midlife yet or think that they have passed midlife at this point. Sustainable personal leadership development and recalibration are a lifelong endeavour. However, it is often the case that the need for recalibration becomes quite acute in midlife.

4.2 Defining midlife

In the first three chapters we have already alluded that as we live longer, the way we experience different stages of life has been evolving. Not only has midlife as a stage of life become more established, some scholars and policy makers have gone beyond and started to also split old age into two categories (see Gilleard & Higgs, 2005): 'old age' (adults over 65 years and relatively healthy and functioning) and 'very old age' (for adults aged 80+ and generally more fragile). Without diving into the semantics of old age and its terminologies, our point is to demonstrate that longer lifespans have challenged us to think differently about the various periods of our lives. In our research and practise it is clear that midlife has become longer, fuller and more meaningful than ever before. Therefore, it is critical we explore what midlife means and why it is important for sustainable personal leadership in the context of increased longevity.

Conceptualising midlife is not an easy task. When we look at the literature it is evident that the way midlife is framed varies according to who is defining it and for what purpose (see Gordon et al., 2002). This is an important point to make because it highlights that we cannot understand midlife without having clarity around the lens we are using. For example, let's take a chronological approach and assume that midlife can be determined by comparison to a standard, such as life expectancy. Although this measure is different across regions, class, gender, the trend is absolute: in 1950, average world life expectancy was 47 years, and in 2020 it was 73.2 years. We shall use 50 years and 75 years, to simplify our numbers. If we define that midlife refers to the part of adulthood before 'old age' sets in, say the part of life which is between 50%-80% of lifespan, then midlife in the 1950s would be that period between 25–40 and midlife in the 2020s would be that period between 37.5–60. Even though the maths seems correct, this chronological approach does not make sense here. While we grow older in much better shape than previous generations, it is probably safe to assume that a 25-year-old in the 1950s did not believe they were middle-aged. In fact, the life expectancy was lower not only because we had shorter lifespans but also because many people did not live past their 50s – thus, skewing the average. Paradoxically, midlife involved a much shorter transition to a time of illness and decline, rather than a period of life in its own right, before old and very old age (see Gilleard & Higgs, 2005).

Many authors writing about life stages (e.g., Levinson writing about the seasons of a man's or woman's life; Erikson psychosocial) have tried to define when midlife happens. An age range of between 40 to 60 years old, or similar, is usually accepted as midlife. However, we would like to keep the boundaries of when midlife begins and ends a bit malleable in this book. Sociologists such as Anthony Giddens (2001), Mike Featherstone and Mike Hepworth (1991) suggest that, in post-modern society, age is defined by the individual. This means that there is no universal definition, and chronological indicators can only tell us so much about being a 'midlifer'. This is illustrated by evidence published in a report from the Centre for Ageing Better in the UK (2018). Drawing on data from English Longitudinal Study of Ageing (wave 8) which surveyed over 6,000 individuals aged 50+, the report found that almost three-quarters (72%) did not think of themselves as old while just 13% did. Even among 80–89-year-olds, 63% did not consider themselves old. This is surprising, even if we assume these respondents were healthier and more active than other people of the same age group. This is because, to some extent, age is self-defined based on our experiences, overall health status, phase of life, interests, social norms and expectations around us, and of course, our increased longevity. Karen and Vivian, for example, went to school together. At the age of 44, Karen became a grandmother and Vivian gave birth to her first child. It is quite likely that they will have a different perception of age and will define midlife differently. Likewise, no matter your age, if you feel healthy and fit you may not see yourself as old.

This subjective view on age and life stages, and consequently the extension of the midlife period in years, has been made more complex by the way our industrial societies have developed from the 20th century until now. These societal changes include the rise of consumerism, the greater focus on individuality, the normalisation of diverse lifestyles and the loosening up of expectations around social norms. For example, we do not necessarily stay married if we are unhappy, leave the workforce at a set age of 65 if we are satisfied and engaged, or stay in the same career our whole lives because we made a choice at the age of 18. In many societies, instead, there is encouragement to pursue our purpose and fulfilment. This new perspective of life magnifies the idea that midlife is not a brief transitional stage in between adulthood and old age, but a period that offers great opportunities for reinventions and meaningful achievements.

Despite the rise of midlife as a distinct life stage, and the potential for positive experiences – it is not all plain sailing. Ageism is a real issue, and beyond plain discrimination it runs deep in our unconscious. While external ageism is frustrating, internalised ageism is a silent saboteur. Internalised ageism is that little voice in our minds that tells us we are too old or it is too late to make a change, to enjoy life or be happy. We call this the narrative of decline. In a study on over 50s moving into self-employment, Puhakka (2022) found that while some individuals cherished the opportunity to learn and develop, often after feeling stagnant in their careers, some resisted retraining or investing on a new occupation because they felt too old to benefit from such investment of time, energy and money. Sadly, we are not talking about octogenarians here – these are individuals with a good 20–30 years ahead of them. This example shows how the narrative of decline can be powerful, persuasive, and can potentially direct us to a path of resignation and defeat. So, it is important to be vigilant and challenge our internalised ageism so it does not interfere with our midlife empowerment.

4.3 Change and stability in midlife

The idea that in midlife experiences and decisions can have long-lasting implications is aligned with both life course and lifespan perspectives. For us to be able to take control and shape our present and future, it is paramount we recognise how desirable and unwanted continuities and discontinuities influence what happens next. There are two theoretical lines of thought that can help us to understand the dynamics of midlife: continuity theory and cumulative dis/advantage theory.

4.3.1 Midlife and continuity

According to Robert Atchley (1989; 1999), who researched adjustment in late life, by the time we reach midlife we tend to have a good idea of our lifestyle, activities, values and identity preferences. He argued that seeking to maintain an optimum level of continuity of these defining aspects of ourselves is a common adaptive strategy to cope with changes from midlife onwards. In his Ohio Longitudinal Study of Ageing and Adaptation (OLSAA), Atchley (1999) noticed that although some individuals would let go of certain activities or aspects, those tended to be minor or gradual fluctuations rather than dramatic shifts. In this study, he differentiated between two types of continuities: internal (e.g., attitudes, preferences, personality, identity, skills, etc.) and external (e.g., activities, physical and social environments, roles, relationships, etc.)

Building on the ideas of personal construct psychology, continuity is judged in relation to the perceptions of ourselves and our activities developed throughout adulthood. In midlife, when the ideas that form our self-concept are sufficiently crystallised, external influences and feedback from others will have very little impact on our sense of continuity. Atchley's view is that new components or changes are easily absorbed and incorporated within our identity, and for instance, the loss of social roles may not necessarily affect us because we can adjust to the loss without losing the thread of who we are. Likewise, discontinuity can only be defined by the individual.

Life changes cannot be assumed to cause identity crises automatically. This was clear in Tatiana's Ph.D. research findings (see Rowson & Phillipson, 2020) which suggested that most academics interviewed did not report experiencing any fundamental discontinuity after retirement. While for some this was because there was little change to their routine of reading, writing, and speaking to groups (akin to teaching), while for others the occasional conversation with former colleagues and students was enough to keep that identity alive. Atchley points out, however, that individuals who insist on certain patterns that are no longer possible, due to ill health, disability, or financial circumstances, may struggle to adjust to different life circumstances. Using the same research as an example, a few retired academics struggled to accept they would not enjoy the same level of seniority (in terms of job grade) or would not be paid the same as before retirement leading to feelings of resentment and bitterness.

Critics of the continuity theory argue that it is impossible to maintain continuity, given how unstable life can be at this stage of adulthood and how influential external factors can be to individual arrangements and routines. The COVID-19 pandemic is an extreme example of that. Many individuals who were furloughed or made to work from home had these changes imposed on them. Although many people have since bounced back, there is evidence that others are still living the consequences of this external shock; for instance, they may be still seeking employment or coping with long-term health consequences of COVID infection for many months, if not years afterwards. Atchley rebutted this criticism emphasising that continuity was not necessarily keeping everything unchanged, but experiencing a coherent sense of self even when circumstances fluctuate or gradually change. Here the keyword is 'experiencing', as personal interpretations play a significant role in differentiating continuity from discontinuity.

Continuity theory as an explanation of how we adjust and adapt to changes from midlife onwards is still valid today (see Rowson & Phillipson, 2020). While objective, often externally observable, continuity may vary according to individual circumstances. Subjective interpretations of continuity relate to the ability of individuals to hold their personal narratives together, as exemplified in the findings from Tatiana's Ph.D. This relates to our ability to tell our stories in ways which preserve our self-concept and self-worth. Often this is operationalised through keeping our focus on areas where continuity is more likely and rewarding, while letting go of aspects that no longer play to our strengths and are unlikely to contribute to our life satisfaction. These two processes of narrowing the scope of what really matters to us and accepting change are associated with positive age-related psychological development and maturation. The key message from reviewing Atchley's continuity theory is that this can be used as a strategy for adjusting to the changes emerging in the second half of adulthood. Most people tend to use this strategy without being explicitly aware of it, while others become stuck when they try to maintain something that no longer fits. So, self-awareness and contextual awareness can boost our ability to keep the thread of our personal narratives coherent, regardless of any fluctuations. These processes are essential to sustain our personal leadership capabilities as we age.

4.3.2 Accumulative advantages and disadvantages

While continuity theory emphasises its positive side of maintaining midlife patterns, studies on how inequalities between people develop over time point out a different kind of continuity. Theories of accumulation, i.e., cumulative dis/advantage (see Dannefer, 2018) and cumulative inequality (see Ferraro & Morton, 2016), suggest that individuals who hold an advantage early in life in certain areas such as educational level, financial resources or network of contacts, will be in a better position long term than others who do not hold such advantages. This is the case even when, viewed at face value, these individuals come from identical social circumstances. Not only does having certain advantages in life open up opportunities, but these advantages also accumulate, so the resulting opportunities become exponentially better. For example, someone with better educational levels or more prestigious qualifications is likely to be offered better jobs, with higher income, which in turn may open other areas of advantage. The reverse is also true, that disadvantages also tend to accumulate and direct individuals to a path of setbacks and greater difficulties. Dannefer links this phenomenon with the idea that the rich get richer and the poor get poorer, which can be understood as a form of continuity.

The core idea around how accumulation leads to certain life outcomes is relatively simple to explain. Its mechanisms, however, are complex because these involve interactions between multiple systemic and individual factors. This means that what leads to someone being in a path of disadvantage or advantage is not only attributable to individuals, but also to the ways in which societies or organisations stratify and label people. Yet, understanding how the system works, how much it affects our choices and decisions can be transformative in giving us more control over the outcomes. This process can be initiated at any point in our lives; however, midlife is a particularly good time for us to take control of our trajectories. There are two key reasons for that. Firstly, at this stage we have had enough lived experiences and have knowledge about ourselves, even if we are not completely aware of it, and we are more likely to have reached the level of development that allows us to take a critical perspective of the system we are in. The latter is linked to Kegan's self-authoring mind we introduced in Chapter 2. To simplify understanding these processes, we will start exploring systemic factors and their potential outcomes.

Systemic factors range between the macro level, like social class or educational status, to the micro level within daily life interactions and experiences. They basically work the same way – but given the personal nature of this book we will explore micro level processes first. Let's imagine two children at school, child A is rated very bright and child B hopeless by the teachers. Without denying that there may be a real difference in ability between these two children, it is likely that child A will be increasingly stimulated and challenged to achieve more. Child B, on another hand, may receive support to improve their performance, but this support is likely to be accompanied with an underlying message that confirms their lack of potential. If these messages and labels are reinforced consistently and frequently enough, they are more likely to stick, thus, placing the two children in very different positions of strength. This positioning, or stratification, is something which they may or may not be able to break away from (especially in the case of the disadvantaged child).

Before elaborating this a bit further, let's try another example. Imagine two new trainees joining a consulting firm. In that context and organisational culture, one trainee is immediately perceived as a highflyer and the other as a bit too academic and sleepy. Soon enough the highflyer will be invited to the most challenging and prestigious projects, whereas the sleepy trainee will be assigned more routine tasks. That initial first impression acts as an advantage, that unlocks (or not) opportunities that will, in turn, not only confirm the label but also bring other advantages, e.g., more knowledge, improved skills or enhanced confidence. Over time, the careers of these two trainees will look substantially different if they remain on these paths. While some objects of accumulation are more generic, like health status, others are explicitly bound to the context, as in the example of the two trainees. The organisational culture, norms and expectations, in our example, favour one style over the other. However, it does not mean that in a different context we will find the same evaluation on the trainees' potential. The key point here is that context matters and sometimes this is the only change needed to revert patterns of accumulation.

The pervasive nature of these different circumstances on their own is enough to create diverging life trajectories, yet these cumulative resources or risks are not stable. Life events, intervention or personal agency can lead to deaccumulation of advantage or disadvantage over time. For instance, someone who has been diagnosed with high cholesterol or blood pressure could make enough lifestyle changes to reverse these conditions. Or someone who had a very prestigious degree, which opened the doors to a stable career, may find their skills becoming obsolete if they remain over reliant on that initial advantage. Possessing accrued advantages in one domain also does not guarantee that there will be no disadvantages in other areas of life. For in-

stance, being in good health does not automatically equate to better financial resources, or vice versa. However, having certain advantages may influence the impact of
outcomes elsewhere. For instance, if you are in good health, you are more likely to be
able to work and have an income, or if you have good financial resources, you would
be in a better position to address health concerns.

Individual responses to circumstances also shape these trends for opportunities
or risks. Often those labels become self-fulfilling prophecies, so when we are placed
into a particular category, we are very likely to respond as others expect. This is explained by how much of our self-concept and identity are relational, thus influenced
by context and others. Research on women in professional firms illustrates this dynamic well, as even when we see a 50/50 gender distribution at a junior level, often
enough we see very few women make partner. This is because the culture in such
organisations naturally favours men, giving them an advantage that over time increases the gender gap (see Hayes, 2019). Let's revisit our trainees again; if trainee 2
accepts his position and 'label' (even though this label may not be explicit), they will
be destined to a path of disadvantage or slow career progression unless the circumstances in the company change such that their style begins to be valued. However, if
they believe they deserve more and reject this position, the chances are they will find
an organisational context which gives them a more advantageous position.

How much we are trapped in these trajectories is debatable. Cumulative dis/ad-
vantage scholars like Dannefer argue that only external intervention can help individuals to escape these trajectories, because our insight into the system, our ambitions
and aspirations are already limited by our lived experience and reality. Researchers
supportive of cumulative inequality theory, like Ferraro and others, instead believe
that individuals have greater agency to escape their destiny. The jury is out there as
there is evidence to make each argument persuasive enough. However, as professionals of personal leadership development, we agree with the latter. Our personal leadership model is designed to activate this agency so we can lead ourselves into a better
life through a process of recalibration.

4.3.3 Life trajectories and agency

Kegan, in many of his talks and interviews about adult development, suggests that the
extension of life expectancy brings an amazing opportunity for personal development
and growth. At a minimum, longevity gives us more time to experience different
things, and midlife has become a particularly pivotal stage for us to seize this opportunity. Midlife almost inevitably entails a recalibration of our life perspectives; and it
is natural that at this point many of us will start to examine our life priorities, goals,
and aspirations and seek change in a desire to reconnect with who we truly are. This
view of midlife has been echoed by many authors, including Erikson and Jung already

mentioned in this book, and others such as Daniel Levinson (1978; 1996) and Gail Sheehy (1995).

Despite being a period of personal transformation, very few experience a 'midlife crisis' as popularly thought (Freund & Ritter, 2009; Lachman et al., 2015). Yet, the changes and transitions are not without their challenges. Like any move from a comfort zone to a less familiar territory, midlife recalibrations involve a certain level of uncertainty and confusion, which in turn can trigger a sense of threat or vulnerability. This is because recalibration at this stage is more than making situational, external, changes, such as changing jobs, taking on an exercise routine or eating more healthily. It also involves transitions, thus, internal psychological and emotional processes to adjust to changes, such as reorientating our self-concept, identity and personal narratives (see Bridges, 1980). It is important to note that no recalibration is successful unless we manage the transition aspect well. In fact, making changes is the easy part if we are emotionally and psychologically ready. This readiness involves understanding where we are, our story and identity, thus developing our personal leadership.

Just like in our workshops, we know that we learn as much from other people's stories as from theories and personal reflections. So, we would like to close this chapter with two stories to illustrate the many concepts and ideas we explored here. We will be retelling the late career experiences of two men, Marcus and Harry. Marcus is a pharmacist. He went to a great university and obtained an advanced degree in pharmacy and then opened a drug store (pharmacy) on a high street in a small tourist town. He owned and managed the shop for many years, until economic factors forced him to close the shop. At this time, he was around 50. He took a job as a hospital pharmacist, which involved continued training, and worked for several years in this fast-paced role. He enjoyed the challenge of working in a hospital environment and being part of a team. He did not miss the management tasks involved in running a shop. When he approached an age at which he might be expected to retire, he moved to a different part of the country, one where there was a critical shortage of pharmacists. As a sociable person who liked to work, he took a part-time job as a senior pharmacist for a chain of drug stores. He worked until he was 80.

Harry was an academic. He earned a Ph.D. in political science and worked as a teacher and researcher at several universities. He was successful at winning major research grants and enjoyed his job. At around the age of 50, Harry was diagnosed with Parkinson's disease. He made the decision to join the research division of a large multinational corporate bank, where he could utilise his research expertise but also obtain better health care coverage and job stability. As his medical condition advanced, over a period of many years, his employer was proactive in periodically reviewing and moving Harry into new roles, in which his work was valued and respected, but which allowed for the realities of his health. He worked until his mid-60s before retiring.

Both Marcus and Harry are examples of 'successful ageing at work'. Each of them experienced a decrease in personal resources at around the same period of late career – Marcus of financial resource and Harry of physical health resource, and each of them adopted successful strategies and new career paths. Both ended up in a position where their work was valued, they were paid well and had good health care benefits, and where there were accommodative HR benefits which allowed for flexible schedules and changing work roles as their needs and abilities changed.

However, there was a fundamental difference between them, and this had to do with their internal personal narratives. Marcus had been a shopkeeper and pharmacist. When he lost his shop, he continued to see and define himself as a pharmacist. He upskilled and undertook continued professional development so that he could practice his profession in many different contexts.

Harry was an academic and researcher. After he moved into the corporate environment, although he was utilising his hard-won skills and expertise as a researcher, he saw himself primarily as an ex-academic. He rarely spoke about his current role but would often speak about his past identity as an academic. Both Marcus and Harry, when faced with serious hardships affecting their careers, made smart decisions. They were able to make valuable contributions, and to prepare for better retirements through accessing higher salaries and pension packages. However, Marcus was able to define himself as a pharmacist, and Harry persisted in defining himself in the past tense, as an ex-academic. This may have something to do with their characters, for example with their degree of optimism, and almost certainly was affected in some way by their physical health, but it is clear that the way in which they framed their story contributed to their personal well-being and their sense of self-worth and social identity.

This is an example of how important we are in defining what happens next. We invite you to reflect on how advantages, disadvantages, continuities and discontinuities were translated into the stories of these men; and, in turn, how their late careers were shaped by what they made of it. We can see here that what happens to us is not as important as what we do with it. There is always a choice. To return to our trainees, we can choose to be trainee 1 or allow ourselves to be trainee 2. The circumstances only dictate part of the story, personal leadership is how we shape what happens next.

4.4 The bottom line

In this chapter we started by clarifying differences and overlaps of lifespan (psychological) and life course (sociological) theories and how these can be used in a complementary fashion to help us to understand how our trajectories unfold. We continued to explore how midlife developed as a stage of life. Midlife is more than an age range; it is also linked to how we evaluate ourselves and our personal circumstances. Therefore, midlife can be seeing as a time of opportunities and change, or a time of decline. How we approach it impacts what we get out of it.

We also discussed change and stability in midlife, and how positive and negative continuities become evident over the course our lives. We defended the view that we can take control of our trajectories if we are aware of contextual and individual factors that shape our life outcomes. This chapter closes Part I. The next part and subsequent chapters will take you through our sustainable personal leadership model. Using many examples and reflective exercises, we will be bringing it to life as if you were in our workshop with us.

Part II: **Personal leadership in action**

Chapter 5
Self-awareness

In this chapter we will explore the first part of our model in detail (Figure 5.1). The starting point to establish our purpose and direction lies in understanding who we are. Self-awareness involves exploring the events, experiences, and influences that shape our identity, allowing us to make informed decisions aligned with our true selves. Self-awareness, however, is infinite as we are always developing, evolving and in flux. So, although we start our model here, this is by no means something constrained to the beginning of your personal leadership development. In fact, self-awareness is a constant pursuit, not necessarily a destination. It is the first step on approaching the era of engaged retirement with purpose, with our eyes wide open.

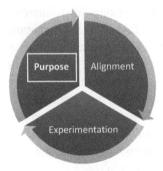

Figure 5.1: Purpose, Sustainable Personal Leadership Model.

5.1 Life stories and identity

In his early career, Dan McAdams (2018) was intrigued by how we manage to keep an integrated and coherent sense of self, given that our identity changes over time and may vary according to the context. For McAdams, it is our life story that brings together our identity and sense of self. Those evolving internal stories or personal narratives allow us to make sense of who we were, who we are and who we are becoming. Thus, we organise our life experiences and events though stories, enabling us to feel whole. This sense making is the mechanism that enables us to successfully pursue meaning and purpose in our lives. As our society becomes more complex and our life trajectories become more individualised, our ability to make sense of our personal narratives is essential to direct our next steps. McAdams refers to this internal storytelling process as narrative identity (see McAdams & McLean, 2013), which is an essential factor in helping us implement positive changes. This is because personal leadership development tends to require us to gain awareness of our meanings, assumptions, and internalised social discourses. Those may impact how successfully we will achieve these changes.

https://doi.org/10.1515/9783111316147-005

Our personal narratives, and our identity, do not occur in a vacuum. We frequently are influenced by our social contexts and our relationships with others. Social discourses concerning what is right or wrong, desirable or undesirable, can become internalised and absorbed into our own personal narratives. Stereotypical norms and expectations concerning matters such as age, gender, social class, or cultural background, can vary from very specific to more broad stereotypes, e.g., 'long hair and mini skirt is only for young women', 'you can't teach an old dog new tricks' or 'older adults are wise'. These societal expectations reflect societal clichés, and when it comes to ageing in particular, these are often negative discourses of decline, ill health and crisis. These can impact how we construct our evolving stories and influence how positively or negatively we view our current and future prospects.

Our relationships, such as those with family and friends, school acquaintances and work colleagues, influence how we construct our self-concept. We form certain ideas about ourselves through social comparison. For instance, if Nick is led to believe he is not very good with change because his siblings coped better with an international move in childhood, Nick may resist or avoid opportunities to work internationally because he is 'not very good adapting to life abroad'. The opposite is also true: Nick could seek international experiences just because he believes he is adventurous in comparison to some external reference. Therefore, our personal narratives are both our own production as much as the production of society and our relationships.

Personal narratives are malleable. Just as we construct this ongoing narrative, we are also able to reinterpret our experiences and rewrite our stories. In a way, this is what talking therapies and coaching help us do. Reviewing our narrative is not only useful for accepting or reinterpreting the past, but also helps us to shape what comes next. Therefore, it may help us avoid the self-fulfilling prophecy trap. This process also allows us to realise how our narratives are framed according to the context and system we are in. So, good and bad, success and failure are never absolute, but are subjected to the norms and expectations within the system we occupy. This is just like the trainees' story we discussed in Chapter 4.

5.2 Our life in chapters

According to our model, personal leadership requires self-awareness. This chapter aims to get you thinking in a deeper way about yourself. We are going to start by introducing an exercise called the Life Chapters Exercise. This exercise, inspired by McAdams' research on narrative identity, has proved popular and a quick internet search would show you that it is used by many people in many different contexts. It is both a thinking and writing exercise, in which the basic instructions are simple: Write the story of your life, in chapters. That quick internet search shows that often this exercise is accompanied by fairly specific instructions about how many life chapters you need, how to bracket them, etc. However, these explicit instructions are detrimental to the aims and usefulness of the task when it comes to personal leadership development and self-awareness.

Although we don't want to give you a detailed structure for this task, we do have some advice about how to best go about it. First, it is intended to be the story of your entire life, thus from childhood. Second, it takes some time to engage properly with the exercise. Therefore, do not assume this is something to write in half an hour. Do some thinking, do some writing, take a break, come back to it, and then maybe sleep on it and re-check the next day to make sure it says what you need it to say.

The story of your life is very personal, and so what you write will be unique to you. So, there is no right or wrong content. The writing process will also be personal, as we all think and work in different ways. You might start by thinking by about how you would 'chunk' your life story. In other words, in how many chapters you will split your 'book'? What would be the organising principle or theme behind each life chapter? What title would each life chapter have? Once you have an idea in mind, start writing. On the other hand, you may decide to start by simply putting words to paper, and let the structure grow organically (and perhaps haphazardly) as you go along. In each of these approaches, there will be some re-arranging and re-thinking about both structure and content, as you write your story.

Of course, being given absolutely no guidance can also be highly frustrating, so let's imagine that this task may take you between 3–6 hours, spread out over a few days, and that you might end up with somewhere between 3–6 life chapters. Don't forget to name your chapters with meaningful titles. You are not writing a magnum opus, or aiming for publication, but you do want to include those things which you think are important to your story. This is your story and your exercise, so you have control over what and how much you say.

The last part of the exercise is to read it aloud. You can read it to someone, a partner or friend perhaps, but the exercise will work just as well if you read it aloud to yourself. We can't over emphasise the power that comes from saying the words aloud. Hearing your voice as you read it is an important part of the experience. We do this exercise in workshops. We give workshop participants the task well in advance so they come to the workshop with their life story written down and they are told in advance that they will be asked to read it aloud to a small group in a session facilitated by us. It takes us an entire morning with groups of 3–4 participants for reading and discussing each person's life chapters. Each time we facilitate these sessions, we are astonished by the power of the exercise, the connections that it makes amongst the group, the depth of perception and self-awareness involved, and the incredible honesty that people bring to this exercise.

We are going to make some observations about the exercise now and give some examples. Personally, we think it is best to do the exercise without any of this discussion filling your head in advance and perhaps influencing what you say and how you say it. Thus, the best way to do the task is to finish reading this sentence, close this book, and go off to write your life story (Exercise 5a).

Exercise 5a:

Imagine your life as a book, its pages filled with the chapters of your experiences. Although the story remains ongoing, there are already distinct and captivating chapters waiting to be explored. Let's divide your life into its significant chapters and provide a brief overview of each. There is no prescribed number of chapters, however, we recommend at least two or three, but no more than seven or eight. Each chapter should be named to capture its essence. You may like to explore the transitions between chapters, highlighting pivotal moments that propel the storyline forward. The style of the narrative is up to you, as this is your book it should resonate with you.

Write the story of your life, in chapters. Take your time!

Welcome back. We hope you enjoyed writing your life story. Did you remember to read it aloud? How did it feel? There are a few things we want you to reflect on.

5.2.1 Chunking and labelling

How we divide our life story into chapters, or chunks, is very revealing. Some people will have chapters that correspond to ages or life stages – childhood, adolescence, early adulthood, etc. If you are someone who has lived in many places, you might have organised it by where you lived at different times of your lives. Kelly often thinks about her life in terms of the four countries she has lived in – America, Australia, Germany, and England. You may have built in a structure based on education and work – primary school, secondary school, university, early career, mid-career. Often, the chapter structure will be synced to major life events like losing a parent, buying a home, and getting married, or to big events that ripple across cultures like war or perhaps the COVID-19 pandemic.

In one of our workshops, a participant – let's call him Carl – had written their life into three life chapters, titled 'Before Alison', 'With Alison', and 'After Alison'. When Carl read his life story, you could feel the profound effect that Alison had on him. Although the relationship with Alison was not prolonged, and although Carl went on to have a number of close, intense personal relationships after the one with Alison, including a happy marriage, Carl felt as if he could track his inner self by how he changed through meeting her. He was one way before he met her, and then knowing her caused him to question everything about his beliefs, values, place in the world, and way of behaving. And everything that followed was predicated on the self that he discovered through that relationship. Thus, the relationship changed who he was on the inside; it changed his self-awareness. I don't think that Carl realised this about himself before doing this exercise.

The way in which your life chapters end up being bundled may be an unconscious process, but how we choose to provide a structure to the flow of our lives says a lot about our identity. This is especially the case when we approach this task from an inside-out perspective on our life, something that may reflect an inner journey unseen to the outside, in contrast to an outside-in perspective, like how a biographer may have chosen to break down your life into sections (Exercise 5b). In both cases, structure can potentially tell us as much as the content of our life chapters.

Exercise 5b:
Reflect and take note on the way in which you chunked and labelled your life chapters.
–   Does it reflect something that perhaps had been hidden or unnoticed?

5.2.2 People and external influences

People who have influenced us often feature heavily in the content of the life chapters. Who were the important people in our lives so far? How did they influence us? This can be a positive or a negative influence. Parents often feature, but also teachers, friends, colleagues. If you read widely, you may have been heavily influenced by writers, philosophers, politicians, artists. The very nature of our identity (see Chapter 4) and the development of our adult minds (see Chapter 2) are highly relational and are influenced by others and by external context. So, as you write this exercise, and as you listen to the life chapters that other people write, you realise that a life story at face value is a series of people, events, and places. However, if we go beneath the surface, it is about accounting for how those people, events, and places have changed you and the way in which you interact with the world. They would not have been part of your life chapters if they did not matter or shape you.

It is also important to reflect on whether you see any underlying patterns of external influences in your life chapters narrative. This can be tricky because they may not be readily apparent. For example, in a workshop, Alex wrote a narrative in which the first chapter focused on his father and their relationship. When reading the story out loud, and speaking with the others in the group, he noticed how much the early death of his father had in fact influenced all of his adult decisions. He unconsciously chose paths which he believed his father would have approved of. In a contrary fashion, Paula told the group how her set of values developed from her family – not by emulating them but by valuing those things which her family did not. Both of them could see a pattern in the decisions they made and how they framed their narratives – one of them conforming to, and one of them rebelling against, family values. There is nothing wrong with being influenced by others, provided that is not detrimental to our sense of self. We can only evaluate that when we are aware of our personal narratives.

Another example is Nancy, and how her narrative reflected a pattern of caregiving. She spent her life caring for others – her parents, her children, her spouse, her community. Being able to see this pattern was useful; it allowed Nancy to reflect on this aspect of herself and make more conscious decisions going forward. Note that those decisions may very well continue to be about caring for others. The patterns you see may reflect old ways of thinking, or they may conform to others' expectations, or to contextual or life circumstances, or perhaps they may demonstrate timidity, or caution, or impulsivity. On the other hand, they may also reflect that you have agency and are happy and self-aware. Seeing a pattern doesn't indicate that you need to change. It provides fuel to your inner dialogue and self-understanding. It brings awareness, which gives you the choice to either keep or change the course of the narrative (Exercise 5c).

Exercise 5c:
Reviewing your life chapters, do you see any patterns emerging? You may like to explore:
- Who are the people featured in different chapters?
- What relationships were critical to your story, negative or positive?
- What have you learned at each stage?

5.2.3 Decision making

One of the interesting things that emerges from this and similar exercises is that there is a real sense that the story of our lives can be seen as a series of decision-making points. You decide what to study in school; should you study engineering or art? You decide where to work; should you take the job in the big company with a bigger salary or stick with the smaller one that offers more autonomy? An opportunity for taking a job abroad comes up; should you move your spouse and kids halfway across the globe, or should you stay where you are and be close to extended family and friends? You've spent 20 years in pharma (or construction, or retail, or real estate) and you really want to try something completely new; do you jump or do you stay? If we look at our life's journey, each point along the way can be framed as a decision.

Decision making is complex and it is one of these areas of research where there is a fair amount of disagreement and, ironically, ambiguity. For instance, in the field of behavioural economics, the book *Thinking Fast and Slow* by Daniel Kahneman (2011) popularised Epstein and Hammond's (see Epstein, 1994) dual process theory. Kahneman refers to the two processes as systems 1 and 2. The first one is a fast decision-making process that can be described as a reflex system, intuitive, based on recognition of patterns associated with mental models (i.e., preconceived ideas, stereotypes or prior experience). Often these kinds of decisions can be associated with those we colloquially call 'gut' decisions, given that the parameters for the decision are not necessarily thought through. The second process, system 2, is more deliberate, analytic, and rational – hence more logical and slower. Thus, we often associate 'head' decisions with system 2. Which is better? The jury is out because there is evidence for both sides. While we tend to make better decisions when we think things through, thus, with our 'head', there is also evidence that when we think too much, we can overlook the signs our 'gut' sends us. So, we may end up rationalising the patterns we noticed unconsciously, playing down their relevance or importance. It is fair to say that we not only need and use both systems, but that while they are perfectly valid ways of making decisions, they are still not bulletproof (see Miller et al, 2005; Cala-bretta et al., 2017). We will refer to these two approaches to decisions as head and gut for the remainder of this section.

In addition to head and gut decisions, there is the idea of 'heart' in decision making. In Kahneman's model, a decision made with the heart would probably fit under system 1, if we think of it as a highly emotionally charged decision. However, we would like to treat it separately here as we broaden the concept of 'heart' decisions, beyond the idea of emotional regulation, to also include decisions informed by our passions, aspirations, or calling. Thus, 'heart' but in a richer way. Therefore, an approach which does not quite fit into the dual process bifurcation of intuitive/impulsive or rational/analytical. While 'passion' has become an overused word, we acknowledge the importance of mak-ing meaningful life choices that are aligned with our sense of self. Yet, passion-driven decisions are not always the best decisions. In the career literature, these heart deci-sions are well articulated in the idea of career calling (Duffy et al., 2022; Hirschi et al., 2019). While pursuing a calling can bring great benefits for our well-being and engage-ment, it can also be detrimental not only to our life satisfaction but also to our health and relationships.

Calling or heart choices may demand a lot more resources from us than less excit-ing head or gut options. Moreover, when these heart decisions fail to give us what we are seeking, the results can be very detrimental to our well-being. Too many of those may be a sign of something else, unfulfilled needs or neglected identities which may be worth investigating. Like head and gut, heart decision making can be either benefi-cial or detrimental to us depending how we use them.

So, let's return to the decisions you may identify in your life chapters (Exercise 5d). It can be illuminating to look at how you make decisions. Do you create lists of pros and cons for each alternative? Do you make a snap decision based on your gut? Do you carefully seek advice from family, friends, colleagues, mentors? Do you agonise over the decision endlessly until time runs out? Do you leave the decision to others and give up agency? Do you think that you are good at making decisions or bad? If you think you are bad at making decisions, do you notice yourself making the same kinds of mis-takes in decision making, for example, always making a decision impulsively or making a decision that is good for other people but maybe not best for you? We often tell people to 'sleep on it' before making a decision; this is in some ways a counter response to impulsivity, but it also has merit in terms of not making big decisions when you are tired.

Exercise 5d:
Reflect on the important decisions you have made. You may like to consider
- Were they driven by heart, head or gut?
- Were they for you or for others?
- Were they about you, or were they made to please/defy other people?
- Which decisions were to move towards something and which to move away from something?
- Can you see a pattern?

5.2.4 Familial patterns and repetitions

It is a common observation that many types of behaviour persist across generations within families. Although these could be repetitions of positive traits and behaviours, like kindness for example, we often discuss this in terms of negative behaviours such as addictive behaviours or abuse. It takes careful acknowledgement of these patterns and exploration of the context, often with the help of a therapist, in order for us to make informed choices to break out of negative family patterns. Sometimes, we are completely unaware of how our behaviours are regulated by habit or by a perception of normality. As we tell our life story, in chapters, we may be able to gain awareness of these familial patterns.

Let's start illustrating our point with a true story which is set during the annual Thanksgiving feast. This North American holiday is celebrated with a large family meal and usually the menu is set and unchanging within a family. The Thanksgiving feast traditionally includes a large roasted turkey as the centrepiece. In this story Mary has been in charge of cooking her family's Thanksgiving feast for decades, having taken over the task from her mother, who took it over from her mother. Mary cooks with her children, who will eventually take over the task. (In this particular example, the traditions and the cooking were passed from mother to daughter; in many families the men also participate in the cooking.)

One year, Mary's daughter asks her 'Why do you always cut off the back of the turkey before cooking it?' Mary stops to think and realises that she doesn't know. 'I do it this way because that's the way my mother always did it.' Mary's daughter turns to speak with her grandmother (Thanksgiving feasts are a multi-generational affair and make this kind of inquiry easy; Mary's mother, Alice, is nearby lending a hand.) Alice thinks about it a moment and says 'That's the way I was taught to cook a turkey by my mother. I don't know why we she did it that way.' Alice's mother is no longer around, but her aunt is, and when they ask the aunt, now quite elderly, about why the turkey is cooked that way, she responds 'Well, we used to cut the back portion of the turkey off and cook it separately. We did this because in those days, ovens were too small to cook an entire turkey. My goodness, do you still do this? How silly is that!'

It is indeed a silly story, but it sheds an interesting light on how it is not only traditions, but also behaviours, habits, and ways of being, expressing, noticing, responding, etc., which are formed at an early stage by our families and environments. They persist without thought even when no longer appropriate or necessary. Sometimes they persist even when they were not healthy in the first place.

These patterns of repetition, often explored in systemic and family therapy, can have a profound effect on our choices. Becoming aware of them gives us the power to break from them when they are not good for us. An example is the one experienced by Rose, who just after a big birthday decided to end her marriage. Talking about this, Rose explained that while she considered her ex-husband a good friend, they were not happy together and there was no love anymore. Their only daughter had already left home at this point and Rose did not want to repeat the experience of her own parents of staying together even when it no longer made sense. Also, for her, there are too many years of life ahead of them to remain in an unhappy situation. The divorce was amicable; Rose maintains a friendly relationship with her ex-husband and feels liberated from the burden of repeating familial patterns.

Although the decision seemed sudden, Rose knew this was something she had to do for a while, yet, given that this was a big change, which could negatively impact others, she was cautious on how to action it. Like Rose, many of us repeat familial patterns that do not work for us, for example staying in a job we dislike, maintaining unhappy or even toxic relationships, neglecting our health, drinking too much, etc. It is not easy to break away, but when we see these patterns, we cannot unsee them and at least consider the possibility of changing things a bit (Exercise 5e).

Exercise 5e:
Reflect on any repetition of familial patterns within your life chapters.
- Can you identify these instances, perhaps without good reason for the repetition?
- Are you continuing someone else's story instead of forging your own?

5.3 Language and narrative

Our personal narratives are not only evident in what we say about ourselves, but in how we say it. Language is an essential part of our inner narrative. It sets the stage, changes our minds, opens our hearts, sets up expectations, impacts us, gives us agency, and makes us human. Language is the crux of our legal systems, our relationships, our understanding of the world, and our knowledge of self. It is powerful, but it also comes with baggage. The content and form in our narratives, conveyed through our language (i.e., words and meanings) shapes our perceptions of self, ageing, career, and change.

Let's start by looking at how we introduce ourselves. Very often, after our name, the first thing we impart about ourselves is our occupation. 'Hi, I'm Helen; I'm a financial analyst' (or sculptor, football player, surgeon, baker, etc.). If you are being introduced at a party, you might hear 'This is Sam, he's my lawyer; Sam this is Abdul, who's an engineer, and Sarah, who's a teacher, and Amrita, who's a surgeon.' As soon as this happens, we have a nice comfortable box to put people in, and we can start making connections and networking, and assuming membership of various types. We not only convey where we belong in such an introduction, but we also are able to make swift category judgements about everyone else. These judgements are of course refined by subsequent knowledge and interaction, but they serve as a starting point to how we present ourselves and how we relate to others.

In some of our workshops, we do an exercise where we ask people to write 20 statements about themselves (Kuhn & McPartland, 1954). These statements are very revealing of our identity, ambitions, interests, social roles and group affiliations. Descriptive statements about character, values, passions, interests: 'I am stubborn', 'I am exactly like my mother', 'I am an adventurer at heart', 'I am never late', are usually found towards the end of the list and often take a bit of thought. The beginning of the list, the part that gets written down first, tends to include groups affiliations and social roles: 'I am a mother', 'I am an accountant', 'I am Portuguese'. Again, these descriptors are usually easy for people to identify. Amongst those, and perhaps because our workshops are often delivered to professionals and executives, occupational roles are almost always at or near the top of the list. This shows how strongly we define ourselves by our work identities. Even when we are not necessarily satisfied or happy with what we do.

In terms of language, words and meaning, what happens when we are uncomfortable for any reason about our work identity, or lack thereof? Then we might say, 'I'm Lana; I am *just* a housewife.' The 'just' word here may be conveying a level of dissatisfaction with the meaning of being a housewife. We also hear longer and more comparative self-definitions: 'I was a lawyer in my native country, but I moved to support my spouse's career, and I can't practice here.' 'I'm planning on being a teacher eventually, but for now I'm in retail.' 'I used to be an engineer, but now I am a stay-at-home mum.' Or 'I'm really an actor, but of course, it doesn't pay the bills, so I work as a bartender.' Notice the difference between 'I'm a bartender', and 'I work as a bartender'. These assert different things. In all of these cases, we often define ourselves by what we used to do or what we hope to do, as if it has more value and is more explanatory. It gives the message 'I am currently doing x, but you should identify me as doing y, because I actually belong in that other box.'

Even in retirement, many of us continue to present ourselves with our work identities centre forward. 'I was in management for a long time, but now I volunteer and do a bit of consulting.' 'I'm retired now, but I used to teach geography.' 'I was a professional gardener for most of my life, but now I dabble in it for fun.' When we no longer work, our work identities are still those we feel most comfortable presenting to the world, and they often take precedence over other types of group affiliations or personal characteristics. Notice, however, that in these cases, our use of language has fundamentally changed: We are defining ourselves using past tense. Let's stop and think about that for a minute. What are the implications of your self-identity when you use the past tense to convey it? Does it mean that you don't value your current identity? Do you fear lack of acceptance? When we use the past tense to describe ourselves are we subconsciously giving permission to others to marginalise us? Or is this because we have not yet settled on our new identities? The answers to these questions are highly personal.

We should also notice the use of the word 'but' in those statements: 'I used to do x, but now I do y'. Why do we feel the need for such qualifications? Even more troubling is that by using this language, we define ourselves by what we are not, rather than by what we are. While the examples we used revolve around work, we observe the same when we describe other aspects of ourselves that, over time, are not completely aligned with our identity and personal narratives.

In midlife many of us will develop positive inner narratives, and therefore, a positive outlook in life. However, negative narratives around failure, decline and loss are not uncommon. For example, 'I used to be on top of my game, but no one wants to employ someone at my age', 'I use to be fit, now it's all downhill', 'I just turned 50 and I feel at my absolute prime professionally and intellectually', 'I finally have the confidence to be myself and have found my tribe'. Our personal narratives are not necessarily objective. A good life on paper may not translate into a positive identity in midlife and vice versa. Some may downplay their achievements and overemphasise unrealised goals and aspirations; others may prioritise positive experiences. Our biography, attitudes around ageing, life and our own self-esteem and efficacy often come together to shape our midlife narratives. And this narrative will very much influence the rest of our lives, decisions we make, and opportunities we are able to seize. Thus, our personal narratives play a big role in our ability to live the good life and to age successfully.

We express our personal narratives in the same way we express our attitudes towards all sorts of things, through the language we use. We would like you, the reader, to become more attuned to the power and meaning of language in preparation for the next sections of this book. You can start by simply observing others' speech, which is often easier than observing our own in everyday conversation. You can also start to notice other forms of communication: documents, news articles, etc., for the language used to discuss different issues.

5.4 Narrative frame and storyline

Notice that your story contains more than just a recitation of events. It is told with a particular voice – your voice – and it reflects decisions that you have made – consciously or not – about how to frame your story. For example, in Nancy's case, the frame she gives to her narrative of caregiving is a critical part of understanding herself. When writing it, she may have presented herself as a victim of other people's expectations who was never allowed the freedom to make choices for herself, or perhaps she presented herself as a practical person who made conscious decisions to care for others because she had the skills and abilities to do so. Or it could have been framed in many different ways. During the part of the task in which you read your story out loud, the framing would be obvious, and the conclusions that Nancy might reach from this could be very deep.

An interesting way to think about the framing might be to compare a memoir to a biography. The first is a personal narrative of one's life, which will reflect both what the author deems important and what they want to project out to the world. It is what we call an inside-out viewpoint. A biography is an account of your life written by someone else. It will reflect what the author deems to be the important aspects of your story, and will reflect their interpretation of your character, impact, and legacy. The framing will be distinctive. A biography will be an outside-in viewpoint; that is, it will represent what someone else thinks of you. The inside-out and outside-in views can be reasonably close or could be quite distinct which demonstrates that there are always many versions, or lenses, to the same stories. So, we think it is important to explore other possible stories and perhaps start by examining if there are any gaps between your inside-out vs. an outside-in version of your story. You can also play with the idea of 'what if . . . .' to challenge your own interpretation of your story, your assumptions, positioning, role, plot and storyline. When we do this exercise and eventually change our personal narratives, we are doing what we call reframing.

Here is an example of framing. Julia has always had this nagging feeling of being an impostor. She enjoyed a fairly stable career in banking and progressed well to a mid-management position. She always joked about how she progressed, saying that she was lucky or that this was a result of administrative errors which ended up favouring her. Deep down, she felt she didn't deserve to be in the position she was, and very often she communicated that consciously or unconsciously. It is likely that if Julia wrote down her life chapters, we would see her narrative of 'an impostor who happened to have been lucky' in many if not all her chapters, from as early as her childhood or adolescence. Her mentor, Brian, who had received coaching training, noticed this persistent narrative frame and called it out during a session. He helped to bring this narrative to Julia's awareness and discussed the implications for her personally and professionally. Brian guided Julia to challenge her assumptions and to find evidence that she is not an impostor, but instead that she is very competent and diligent with her work and progressed because others can see her value. Julia reflected a lot on this session and since then she no longer feels like an impostor. However, Julia, out of habit, still sometimes refers to herself as if she were an impostor. Although she does not believe that, changing her habitual undermining language and narrative framing will still require deliberate effort and commitment.

Our narratives, when they are framed in a way which empowers us, give us more agency and are a great tool to get us what we seek. Even when we have a positive narrative, there are moments we need to at least tweak the narrative to help us to move into a new life stage, new context or start another adventure. Research shows that for us to truly redirect our paths, change behaviours or let go of certain habits, shifting the narrative is essential. This principle goes beyond the purpose of personal or career development but is also true for any lasting behavioural change at a population level and the successful implementation of public and social policy initiatives, like stopping smoking, starting exercising or wearing seatbelts (Wilson, 2011). Editing our stories, especially our personal narratives, re-shapes our identity (see McAdams, 2018), which in turn will influence our subsequent perceptions, choices and actions (Exercise 5f). Julia's frame of an 'impostor' may have cost her some good stretch assignments or opportunities, which she may have turned down. By no longer adopting the impostor frame, Julia can see herself achieving much more and this belief alone will impact what happens next for her, as a positive self-fulfilling prophecy.

It is worth noting that there are circumstances in which a positive narrative can be detrimental to us. When we are using a positive narrative to play down a dysfunctional reality, such as workplace bullying, excessive drinking, unhealthy lifestyle, etc., the positive frame prevents us from taking appropriate action. This is important because the damaging effects will emerge eventually or indirectly. So, for instance, when Sam accepts that he has been a target of bullying at work, he is able to consider the necessary steps to change his situation. This does not mean to embrace the victim narrative, but instead to proactively do something about it Even if that means changing jobs.

Exercise 5f:
Read your life chapters again as if you were reading a novel, try to identify the following:
-   What character are you playing (e.g., victim, hero, villain)?
-   What is the main plot? And the genre (e.g., comedy, tragedy, romance)?
-   What are the critical moments, turning points, climaxes?
-   How are these usually resolved?

If, upon reflection, you aren't happy with your framing, how would you re-frame it?

5.5 Personal values and priorities

Looking at your life story and personal narratives will help you to better understand yourself. This self-awareness will feed into the model for sustainable personal leadership and will guide you in making sensible decisions for your career and more generally for your well-being. This process of self-reflection, if done with any diligence, will inevitably dig down to a basic level of beliefs and values. What do you believe in?

How do you know what the right/wrong thing to do is in a given situation? What is important to you? If you think back to your life chapters narrative, you may have written the entire narrative without explicitly addressing values, but if you look between the lines at what you selected to write about and what you didn't, and at the impact that various events have had on you, you will probably be able to see your values are instrumental to your story.

Our values are intangible – we can't see them; although we can see our behaviours, which are, in the best possible world, aligned with our values. In workshops, we often ask people 'What is a value?' Some of the answers seem to be consistent across workshops and groups: A value is something that is learned as a child, from our family or community. While values can change, they tend to be fairly immutable. Values act as guides to our behaviours. Our values help us distinguish between right and wrong. Despite the general feeling that we know what a value is, it turns out to be hard to verbalise it. This is partly due to the fact that it can get mixed up with your notions of 'belief', ethics or morality (what is 'right' and what is 'wrong').

As academics, we like to have explicit definitions for every term we use. One of the classic academic definitions of a value is found in Kluckhohn (1951, p. 95): 'A conception, explicit or implicit, distinctive of an individual or characteristic of a group, of the desirable which influences the selection from available modes, means and ends of action.' Depending on your lens, be it from sociology (as with Kluckhohn), pop psychology, philosophy, religion or your parent's teachings, the definition will be different, but the concepts of character, of personal and community beliefs, and of ethics (right and wrong) will likely form the core.

One of our colleagues, Kevin Money, an expert on corporate social responsibility and reputation, described values in an interesting way during a workshop: A value is something that makes your stomach hurt when you cross it. This was in the context of comparing the values of an organisation you work for with your own personal values and checking for alignment or misalignment. The point is simple: If you do something that goes against your values, you feel it in your gut. It turns out the gut is a fairly accurate arbiter of what matters to you, and of the innumerable compromises we tend to negotiate with ourselves every day.

You may be asking, why is this important? Our values are a fundamental aspect of self-awareness and important for us to make sense of who we are. Knowing our values helps us to understand our motivations, to be true to ourselves, to make better decisions, and to learn, grow and live with purpose. This deep self-knowledge, combined with a willingness to adapt and develop, allows us to act with honesty and integrity, and to follow the courage of our convictions.

In the real world, we may find that our values are often at odds with each other and we must make compromises. For example, you may value honesty, and you may also place value on not causing anyone hurt. You may easily excuse a 'white lie', for example telling someone that you loved the cake they baked for you, rather than hurt their feelings and tell them it was dry and flavourless. While this example may seem simple and straightforward, we make compromises with our values all of the time, and some may have greater consequences. Our values play an important role in how we set our life priorities. This becomes increasingly evident as we mature and naturally feel more compelled to become our authentic selves and live a more meaningful and purposeful life (see Chapter 2).

While we can say that values are relatively stable, priorities will change according to our circumstances and our resources. Many of us may have experienced a time when we realise that our priorities are no longer relevant or working for us; instead of allowing us to flourish, they are a distraction to what really matters. Nilesh's top priority for many years has been to provide for his children, both in the material and the emotional sense. This stemmed from his strong family values and the desire to be there for his children. He has made decisions that allow him to focus on this, for example, turning down opportunities for travel and for increased responsibility at work. This year Nilesh's youngest child goes off to university; he and his wife will be 'empty nesters'. This provides him with an ideal time to reset his priorities; he can take opportunities for himself. Nilesh may decide to pursue some form of higher education himself, or to take on a strategic leadership position, or maybe to switch gears and move to an entrepreneurial role, or to take up scuba diving. The point here is that while Nilesh's priorities have changed, his values have not.

Perhaps you notice that your priorities could use a re-set. Maybe you have focused so much on career and financial advancement that you have sacrificed family time and caring responsibilities. Perhaps your health situation has changed, and you need to re-evaluate. The COVID-19 pandemic is credited with a mass re-evaluation of priorities around lifestyle, working arrangements, and retirement, which caused both personal and societal upheavals. Our values help to act as a compass, and the periodic recalibration of our priorities can help us to feel more aligned and to flourish. It is perhaps a cliché, and certainly an oft-repeated plot point in popular culture, that it is only when we are faced with the threat of a near-death situation or trauma, that we understand what is important to us. One point we often make in our workshops is that the best time to think about what is important to you is not when you are running from a burning building, but rather when you are in a safe, comfortable, reflective space. It is definitely an easier way to do it. Thinking about your values and what is important for you right now should lead naturally to examining your priorities.

Remember that taking care of your own health and well-being should be an important priority. We spend much of our adult lives as caretakers – caring for our children, parents, extended families, friends and communities, but also for the organisations we work in. We devote ourselves to careers, as much to be able to provide for and support those we care about, as for our own satisfaction and engagement. For many of us, the pressure to perform and produce in order to provide becomes ingrained, and we forget that priorities can and should change as circumstances change. Social expectations tell us that it is selfish to put ourselves first. It takes courage to question your assumptions, and to recognise when it is time for change. It takes courage to prioritise yourself and to make decisions that enable you to protect your health and well-being. In Chapter 7, we will explore some tools that can help you to periodically recalibrate your priorities and make use of the resources available to you to make sustainable choices.

5.6 Personality

Most of you will have taken a personality test at some point in your lives. For example, the Myers-Briggs Type Indicator (MBTI) is widely used by both companies and individuals to provide insight into personality. Many people will know their MBTI 'type'. Or perhaps you have experienced other tasks, such as a five factor personality assessment, emotional intelligence test, or career strengths inventory, etc. These tests can provide us with interesting fuel for thought, and a vocabulary for us to examine some of our assumptions, preconceptions, attitudes, and behaviours. If used in this way, they can be interesting and can start off an internal dialogue which may be helpful.

However, personality tests, by their very nature, assign labels to us. And once you have been assigned a label, you often end up in a box, which can be problematic. For example, the MBTI differentiates four distinct categories with opposing labels. One of these is introversion or extroversion. How many of you have been labelled as an introvert or an extrovert by MBTI? If your company uses MBTI results to assign you to different functions within the organisation or as a template against which to compare results, then being classed as either an introvert or an extrovert may fundamentally change your career trajectory because you will be assumed to be better at certain tasks than others and will be channelled into pre-determined directions.

Worse still is when we apply these labels to ourselves and use them to put ourselves into a box, limiting what we can achieve. If you believe you are an introvert, for example, then you may pass up opportunities for team leadership or public speaking because you believe your talents lie in working quietly in the background. *Quiet*, by Susan Cain (2013) is a thought-provoking book, which looks carefully at the leadership power to be found in what we might normally label as introverted personalities. It demonstrates that not only may the box be wrong, but the label on the box may also be wrong.

It is also important to note that although we may have some traits that are fairly consistent, each of us responds in different ways according to context, and thus describing ourselves as either/or, instead of on a fluctuating continuum, also diminishes the reality of our characters. You may exhibit introverted characteristics when meeting your new partner's extended family but exhibit extroverted characteristics when leading your team at work. So, be careful of putting too much confidence in personality types. Use them as a starting point for introspection, perhaps, but try to tease out the contexts in which different characteristics come into play. You may have guessed by now that we will not be testing or suggesting any particular model of personality.

Instead, we encourage you, using your own words, to reflect on your preferences and how you may come across.

Personality types, traits, and labels try to answer the question about what makes you 'you'; in other words, what are your special or unique characteristics, and how do those compare across groups? Another way that you could approach this is through reflection. We have already mentioned in this book the concept of inside-out versus outside-in perspectives on self. The inside-out view is generated from within, it is the 'you' that feels authentic to yourself, the person you are on the inside, it is your conception of 'self' that may cut across life domains and social roles. The outside-in view is generated from without; it is the 'you' that others see in a particular context and based on the value system of that specific environment. This outside-in view can feel 'imposed' on you and comes complete with labels, and all that those convey. These two may be closely aligned or wildly out of touch with each other; for most of us, the truth is probably somewhere in the middle.

In our workshops we sometimes ask the question 'What is special about you?' (Exercise 5g). The way we answer this can help to tease apart the inside-out and outside-in views (see Dalton, 2021). What do we think, from deep within ourselves, is special, interesting, or unique about us? What traits, abilities, characteristics, behaviours do you see? You may be good at projecting these out to the world, or you may keep them more or less hidden. The outside-in answer to the question 'What is special about you?' is one that would emerge if you asked other people to answer this question. If you asked your boss or your colleagues, or your spouse or friends what is special about you, what would they say?

> **Exercise 5g:**
> What is special about you? Use the inside-out view and don't be shy to express yourself.

5.7 The bottom Line

In this chapter, we have focused on the first element of purpose: self-awareness. We have utilised the life chapters exercise to start this process, and from there have examined many different things that contribute to your sense of self – life experiences, family expectations, decision making, framing, people who've influenced you, personal values, personality. We have talked about how to re-frame narratives, set priorities, explore your purpose as well as how to recognise patterns and expectations (yours and others) that may be keeping you stuck. We will now move to explore the next aspect of purpose, our professional identity.

Chapter 6
Professional identity

The previous chapter was focused on self-awareness and personal identity. Here we want to explore the second element essential to purpose (Figure 6.1); thus, our professional identity. You may already have a good concept of your professional identity; in fact, for many of you it may be easier to think about your professional identity than your personal one, because it is the one we spend a lot of time in, and have invested time and effort into developing. Therefore, it is important that we explore this one now that we had the chance to reflect on who we are first. Understanding the dynamics of personal and professional identity allows us to navigate opportunities, decisions and choices more purposefully.

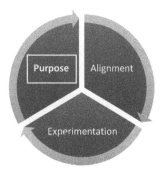

Figure 6.1: Purpose, Sustainable Personal Leadership Model.

6.1 Professional vs. personal identity

You will probably be fairly practised at picking up your professional identity, say, when you walk into the office or slip on a jacket to take a zoom call, or when you attend a professional gathering; and may also recognise that feeling of shrugging it off at the end of the day, when you revert to being 'you, the person'. If you relate with that feeling of pulling on and off your professional identity, then you will also know that these two identities do not 'feel' the same. Perhaps you feel more relaxed and approachable outside of your professional self; maybe you feel more confident at work than outside of it. For many of you, it may be the opposite; perhaps you have some degree of impostor syndrome on the job but feel good in your skin outside of work. You may have different attitudes and behaviours about teamwork and collaboration, for example, in your professional and personal lives.

One of the consequences of thinking about your personal and professional identities in a focused way is that you may begin to see that they are not aligned. Note that we are not suggesting that the desired state is to have perfect alignment between your

https://doi.org/10.1515/9783111316147-006

professional and personal identities; in fact, for many of us the differences between these two allow us to function better. Marla, for example, is an air traffic controller. At work, she must always be 'on'. She has to stay focused, in control, professional, and cool in a crisis. Lives depend on her ability to think fast and make decisions. When she is off work, she enjoys being 'off'. She is famous among her friends for being very easy-going; she likes to go with the flow and let other people make the decisions. Marla knows that her ability to switch off the focus while off the job, helps her to keep her focus sharp while on the job. She sees this not as a misalignment, but as a healthy coping strategy to an intense work environment. There are, however, some areas in which a lack of alignment may become quite difficult to maintain; for example, if your personal values don't align well with your professional identity.

One thing that may impact on the relationship between these two is the centrality and importance of your work identity relative to your personal identity. Do you define yourself as a person based on your professional identity? Is it the basis of your self-esteem? The answer to these questions is probably not 'yes' or 'no', but somewhere in the middle. However, if the answer is more closely aligned with 'yes', then the notion of retirement, or of midlife transition or career change is likely to be especially daunting. As you work through this chapter, we will help you to gain a clearer perspective on your professional identity. We will discuss career goals and patterns, how to recognise your 'superpowers', how to let go and move on from unrealised plans that may be keeping you stuck in place, and also about meaningful work. We will help you develop a personal and professional compass that will help guide you as you make decisions.

6.2 Professional brand

Let's talk about professional brand. At a broad level, your brand is the thread that underlies and connects your career path. It is not the same as saying 'I am a psychologist' or 'I am a lawyer' as the reality of your professional persona is much wider and encompasses many different types of tasks. Being able to recognise and articulate your professional brand is an important part of understanding your professional identity.

Here is an example. Leonardo da Vinci is usually described as an artist (albeit a great one). However, we know that he was also a gifted engineer, an inventor, an architect, a scientist, and an anatomist. If we try to think of his professional brand, we might say that he was a problem solver. In all of his endeavours he was excited by the challenge of solving problems, whether it be one of capturing perspective on canvas, building a bridge, or imagining flight. He was also a polymath, that is, one who has studied and is knowledgeable about many different fields of knowledge. This contributes to his brand as well, as it feeds into his problem solving; for example, his knowledge of anatomy brought insight to his art, but also to his engineering.

You don't have to be a Leonardo Da Vinci to have a professional brand; we all have one, whether it is articulated or not. Let us say that you have made your career in sales. You have moved companies a few times and have made your way up the ladder and have a reputation of delivering targets. Your brand is not likely to be 'I am a salesperson' or even 'I am a great salesperson'. Your professional brand will reflect the things about you that enable you to be good in your role. For example, your brand may reflect your deep understanding of product and market, your ability to listen, your people skills, your ability to strategize, your drive, your perfectionism, or a combination of these or other skills and abilities and personal traits that contribute to your professional identity. It will enable you to distinguish yourself from others in your professional milieu. Note that it will also help you to identify those qualities that would allow you to work effectively in other professional contexts.

Why is this important? Well, being aware of our brand allows us to talk about ourselves, what we do and why. Understanding your brand allows you to be authentic. Ari, for example, is a capable business leader, who has gained a reputation for taking over failing companies and turning them around. He knows that his value lies not in understanding every aspect of the business, but in knowing how to choose the right people and in allowing them the leeway and authority to do their jobs. Because he knows where his strength is, he doesn't need to pretend to be an expert. He can ask questions, be curious, and admit ignorance without tarnishing his brand.

Authenticity is a common buzzword these days in business and leadership, but that does not diminish the power of being authentic. Understanding our brand also allows us to transfer from one role to another, and from one place to another because we know the brand 'value proposition'. We often tend to get stuck thinking about ourselves within a particular context. However, most of us have developed skills and knowledge that are transferable to other contexts, industries, and roles. Take Emily, for example. She got a job right out of college, working for a large, busy restaurant. Ostensibly, she was in charge of booking tables and manning the front desk, but her talent for organising led to her transforming all aspects of process management, from seating, serving, ordering, staffing, and scheduling. By chance, she managed to be offered a job on a movie set, where she soon had applied her organisational skills to every aspect of site management. From there, she worked for a glass manufacturer, a local crafts council, and then a busy hospital critical care centre. When Emily describes her brand, she doesn't say 'I understand restaurant management', or 'I manage film sites'; she knows that her value doesn't lie in her knowledge of glass manufacturing, or local crafts or of critical care. It lies in her ability to visualise a process as a gigantic puzzle with many moving pieces, and to see, articulate, and implement solutions. Digging down into your brand, understanding your professional identity and your value as a professional, will open up new contexts. Note that you don't have to change career contexts frequently, like Ari and Emily, in order to have a transferable brand. Even if you have spent 40 years within a single working context, within a family-owned company, perhaps, or within the HR department of a single large corporation, you will still have a professional brand and a skill set that can be put to use in many varied contexts (Exercise 6a).

Exercise 6a:
Let's take some time to examine this concept of brand as it applies to you.
- What do you think is your brand? Have a go at writing it down; You may like to use insights from the previous chapter such as what is special about you.
- When you were a child what did you want to be/do?
- You may or may not want to revise this at the end of the chapter.

Thinking about brand is one of those areas where it is good to apply some creative thought and have some fun (Exercise 6b). Remember also that brand is fluid; it can and will change over time. It is also closely linked to reputation. While not something that you may have total control over (especially with respect to the outside-in aspects of brand), you do have control over the way that you think about yourself and how you act in a professional context.

Exercises 6b:
- Which advertising tagline from a known brand could you use to describe your professional self? Does it tell you something about you? As an example, compare taglines for Ford 'Built to last' to BMW 'The ultimate driving machine'. The former emphasises reliability and the latter emphasizes performance. The tagline differentiates one brand from another as with Apple's 'Think different' which is often seen as a response to IBM's 'Think'. Which known brand tagline would most closely describe your professional brand?
- Make a list of the things which you do in your professional capacity which could be transferred into different professional contexts. For example, a journalist might have a list that includes 'research facts, interview people, consolidate data, engage stakeholders, write well, be meticulous, work under time pressure, understand nuance, be curious' amongst others.
- Imagine that you are moving to a new country and starting up a new life, untethered by the old. If you could choose a professional brand in this new context, what would it be?

We hope that these questions and exercises have got you started thinking about your professional brand, and perhaps in bringing some creativity to that endeavour. Let's put this aside for the moment to examine your career patterns and work history. Note that we will cover several exercises and points that will come together towards the end of this chapter; this notion of brand will continue to percolate as we look at other aspects of career and professional identity.

6.3 Career patterns and work history

We have just spent some time thinking about your professional identity and brand, but without any examination as to how you got there. Now, let's examine those decisions and events that brought you to where you are now, and make some observations about underlying patterns. To begin with, we will utilise three separate exercises aimed at exploring the past and present.

6.3.1 Career timeline

The first exercise we want to pursue is the timeline. You are undoubtedly familiar with timelines – they are a visual tool for organising events according to their occurrence in time. They can be used for many purposes, for example, in project planning and management, but here we will be using it as a means to record the events that are instrumental to your story so far. As it is your personal timeline, you can include in it whatever you wish, but make sure to include those events which have influenced your career decisions and have resulted in you being where you are now professionally. When we use this exercise in workshops, we point out that a personal timeline like this often contains two different kinds of information. It will likely include major milestones – births, graduations, marriages, deaths. These are the types of milestones that might be recorded in a government registry office; they are usually publicly available, and mark socially significant and recognised milestones. A different type of information that may end up on your timeline is an event which has been critically important in your development or has impacted on you greatly, but which may not be obvious to others, or that perhaps is not as meaningful out of context.

As an example, in career workshops we sometimes share a timeline of Albert Einstein's life. It contains those milestones you would expect: when he was born, married, graduated from university, won the Nobel Prize. It also contains some unexpected events. Einstein claims that he was given a compass when he was five years old, and that this event set in motion his fascination with time and space that eventually resulted in his theory of relativity. This event 'given a compass' is included on the timeline, as Einstein viewed it as a critical event in the development of his thinking.

Do you have such events or moments of understanding that have influenced your path? Many workshop participants find that they can identify such events. Minh, for example, in drawing her timeline, recognised how her mother's early death from a rare illness set her on the path to studying immunology and genetics. Martin credits a year in Japan after university as fundamentally changing his goals and at a deeper level, his understanding of self. Peter had a heart attack at the age of 50 which encouraged him to make a change in career to one that was less stressful. After a hurricane devastated local communities, Roberto came out of retirement to coordinate relief activities, and eventually created a new career in community organising. Sam included on his timeline a fundamental conversation he had with a friend that opened his eyes to some bad behaviour on his part and forced him to challenge his assumptions. Manuela got angry when she was passed over for a deserved promotion and quit her job; this allowed her some space to discover what she really wanted to do. These types of things – an illness, a moment of anger, a natural disaster, a frank conversation – might not seem to be a major part of one's story when looking from outside-in.

There are big events, too, which can have very broad impact on society and culture. These may influence you directly in very obvious or in more subtle ways. The COVID-19 pandemic is one such event that had massive global repercussions which have changed the way that many of us work. The 'Me Too' movement is another 'event' which also has had, and continues to have, deep repercussions and a ripple effect across many fields and global contexts. Both or either of these may have impacted on you personally and caused a change in perspective or habit or thinking that represents a fundamental shift in your timeline (Exercise 6c).

Exercise 6c:
Draw a timeline of your life so far, including all the events that influenced you to be where you are now career-wise.

Once you have completed your timeline take note of your reflections, including anything that surprises you. Maybe there was something that you previously didn't consider to be significant, which now feels more important?.

We are asking you to create your own timeline. This is not a CV, so it is from an inside-out perspective. You should include those things which have impacted you and resulted in your arriving to the place where you are now. As we have already explored your life more broadly through your life chapters, here the main focus is on professional identity, thus our examples here revolve around professional impacts. However, it is perfectly fine if you wish to take a broader approach to your timeline.

6.3.2 Career metaphors

Your timeline is another piece of the puzzle of your professional and personal identity. It is a part of the information package we hope you are accumulating as you work your way through these exercises and reflective questions. For now, let's put this timeline aside and move on to another exercise. We want you to think about your career as a whole, up to this point, and to do so, we will use the concept of metaphor. This expository technique is incredibly powerful as metaphor allows you to wrap your ideas in a story or picture that resonates with others. It is one of the reasons why successful business leaders and visionaries use it so often as a means to unify and motivate their followers. Metaphor is also great to help us think outside the obvious, and is a common tool in career conversations.

We have been using metaphor in our workshops and coaching sessions for many years. It is a fun exercise, and at first glance seems quite straightforward, but there is often some very deep context underlying your choice of metaphor, and frequently ambiguity as well. We often ask people to draw their metaphor and find that there is value both in developing/drawing your metaphor and in sharing and talking about it. In particular, it is enlightening to see how many people at midlife have metaphors of being stuck (Exercise 6d).

Exercise 6d:
Think of a metaphor for your career. You may write it down, draw it, storyboard it, perhaps think of a film, book, soundtrack or image that reflects your career metaphor. Be creative!

Together with our colleague, Chris Dalton, we have noticed that the career metaphors produced by our Executive MBA participants tend to be grouped into themes. By examining these metaphor drawings, we have arranged the career metaphors into four distinct categories. Two of these could be defined by the feelings, positive or negative, that the participant currently held towards their career. First, there were metaphors indicating positive growth and clarity; these may include images of flowering trees or butterflies. One MBA participant drew a large pair of eyeglasses and, upon questioning, explained 'Now, I can see clearly.' These metaphors reflected a general level of contentment with the state of one's career. In contrast are the metaphors which indicate frustration and 'stuckness'. There are so many examples of this category, but some include brick walls, quicksand, puzzles, junctions, question marks, and going around in circles. One example from a workshop was a drawing of a person trying to juggle, while on a unicycle, going up a ladder, with people aiming crossbows at them. These metaphors reflect a general feeling of discontent, and in particular of being stuck in one place, or heading in the wrong direction.

The other two categories we identified were focused on the arc of the career itself, rather than on measures of personal contentment. These were distinguished by metaphors in which the focus was more on the journey itself, or more on reaching the end of the journey. The former could be represented, for example, by a drawing of a series of rolling hills or mountains, with a person making their way up and down as they journeyed, perhaps through various landscapes and weathers. The latter may be represented by someone reaching the top of the mountain and planting a flag, or maybe someone crossing the finish line of a race.

Do you recognise any of these themes as being similar to your metaphor? These examples were all drawings, but the exercise will work with any type of creative expression of metaphor. For example, if you chose a film to represent your career, the choice of George Romero's *The Dawn of the Dead* would have a different resonance than Philip Kaufman's *The Right Stuff*. Perhaps you were more *Everything Everywhere all at Once*, or *Catch-22*, or maybe *Bambi*? The same works with music. We all know what feeling the *Jaws* soundtrack invokes, and if someone chose that as a metaphor for their career, we would instantly 'get' it; not in the particulars of the career, but in the feeling of dread and something bad on the horizon. This might seem humorous, but the interesting thing about metaphor is how easily it makes a connection. As soon as we mention one of these films as a career metaphor, it puts a picture in your head.

If your metaphor is one of being stuck, if you imagine yourself endlessly trudging through a quicksand filled jungle, or sitting at a crossroads unable to decide which turn to make, do not despair. It may help to know that this is in fact the most common type of metaphor that was expressed in our workshops and sessions. The members in these groups are primarily midlife successful career people, and many of them are feeling stuck. In fact, for many people, the justification behind pursuing an Executive MBA or some other form of higher education in midlife, or of signing on for executive coaching sessions, or indeed, for picking up a book like this one, is because there is a feeling of being stuck, or at the very least of yearning to 'shake things up a little'. You are not alone in that regard. It may also help to know that there are well-evidenced techniques and strategies for making changes that both suit you and grow with you, and that lead to better health and well-being. That's what we do in this book. And note that even if you have the sunniest metaphor, and feel perfectly placed in your career and life at the moment, this book is still helpful because its goal is helping you to make sustainable decisions for health and well-being as you grow and things change.

6.3.3 Career anchors

Now, let's shift just a bit from the timeline and metaphors to explore some of our career drivers. In the 1960s, Edgar Schein who is famous for his research on organisational culture, started to explore the underpinning reasons why people changed jobs and careers. He identified eight key patterns of motives, values or perceived talents which he labelled as career anchors (see Schein, 1990). Schein believes that we are only able to identify those anchors a few years after we start to work and that we begin to learn about ourselves in the context of work. He differentiates anchors, which will tend to be stable throughout our career, from vocational choices as two distinct aspects of our careers. Finally, Schein argues that we only typically have one main anchor, although he accepts that other anchors can also be important. When we run workshops, this idea of one main anchor is always a subject of debate. Most people can identify at least two or three anchors they believe as very important. However, when we flip the question, from those identified as important to which one, when taken away, would lead you to resign from a job, our participants can often identify 'the one'.

Schein's career anchors are:
1. **Technical/Functional Competence**: Focused on becoming experts in a specific technical or functional area. Individuals with this anchor are motivated by opportunities for mastery and advancement within their field of expertise.
2. **Managerial Competence:** Motivated by a desire for leadership roles and responsibilities. Individuals with this anchor seek opportunities to lead and manage others, as well as to make strategic decisions.

3. **Autonomy/Independence:** This career anchor relates to autonomy and independence in work. Individuals here would prefer roles that allow them freedom to work independently, make their own decisions, and control their work environment.

4. **Security/Stability:** Individuals with this anchor seek job security and stability. They tend to prioritise roles and organisations that offer stability, predictability, and long-term employment.

5. **Entrepreneurial/Creativity:** This career anchor reflects a desire to be creative and innovative. Individuals with this anchor prefer roles where they can take risks, pursue new ventures, and generate novel ideas or products.

6. **Service/Dedication to a Cause:** The desire to make a positive impact and contribute to a meaningful cause or mission is central to this anchor. Here individuals seek roles that align with their values and allow them to serve others or advance a greater purpose.

7. **Pure Challenge:** Intellectual or physical challenges are at the heart of this career anchor. Individuals are motivated by roles that push their limits, require problem-solving skills, and offer opportunities for personal growth and development.

8. **Lifestyle:** Here the focus is achieving a balance between work and personal life. Individuals with this anchor prefer roles that allow them flexibility and scope to pursue personal interests outside of work.

Research on career orientations did not challenge Schein's ideas around anchors but highlighted the importance of being less deterministic when applying it to current context of career and applying it across cultures. Career orientations, as Rodrigues and colleagues (2013) prefer to call them, may include aspects Schein may have missed. This is because these orientations are context-specific, meaning they are shaped by the person's work environment and culture. They found that, often, individuals have a primary and a secondary orientation. These orientations are not strictly stable, as they may become more or less salient with time, ageing and changing life circumstances. So, they are very much like any other aspects of our identity and personal narratives that may adaptively change over time. Despite these caveats regarding Schein's career anchors, we still find these a useful tool to explore career preferences and orientations (Exercise 6e). This is especially the case when we combine any insights with the ones emerging from exploring career timeline and metaphors.

Exercise 6e:
Using Schein's career anchors as an inspiration, can you identify what is the main driver of your career? What is the aspect that if taken away would push you to resign? Take note of instances where this was evident to you.

6.3.4 Career patterns

Now that we have explored your career timeline, your metaphor, and your drivers it is time to step back and examine the emerging trends. Considering this complex picture composed of a series of decisions, jobs or roles, your drivers, can you see any patterns? There may be an obvious pattern that leaps out at you, but it is likely that it will be more subtle, and you may need to reflect more deeply and perhaps to question some of your assumptions about yourself to find any.

Let us give you some examples of what we mean here by a pattern. Susan had an a-ha moment in a workshop: 'Every choice I've made has been one to distinguish myself from my family. They are flighty and creative and have messy lives; I strive for order and want things that are black and white. I want to be seen as a serious person.' Felix hates taking advice. He has a habit of always defying authority, sometimes just for the sake of it. He is hot-headed. When he looks at his career pattern, he finds that he often makes decisions quickly without thinking things through carefully. He often regrets these decisions and has made a lot of job changes. Jing doesn't like to take risks. When she looked closely at her work history, she found that she had many opportunities to try something new and take on major responsibility, but she tended to stay with the safe and secure. Sandra likes the new and shiny. She has great ideas and lots of drive, and is good at starting things, but once that is done, she is ready to move on. Ibrahim just puts his head down and works. He avoids personality clashes, he tries to please his boss, he stays out of office politics, and every three or four years he moves up a rung on the corporate ladder. Marnie agonises over every decision. No matter what she chooses to do, she wonders if it was the right choice. She is so focused on past opportunities, she doesn't enjoy where she is. Samuel likes to roll the dice; every decision he makes is completely spontaneous. He may not always make a good decision, but he has lots of fun and never regrets anything.

Each of these explorations is a piece of a puzzle and together, they provide necessary information needed for a more informed self-awareness (Exercise 6f). The insights from reflecting on your professional brand, your timeline, your career metaphor and your career anchors, within the context of your personal narrative, help you to make better career decisions and pursue the right opportunities (not necessarily because they are socially accepted or expected).

Exercise 6f:
Reviewing the outputs of your career timeline, metaphor and anchors, what patterns do you notice? You may like to consider:
- How did your choices come about? Accidental or pursued?
- Were there others involved in these choices?
- How much have you pursued your own career orientation?
- Have you pursued paths in order to please others?

Identify 1–3 key factors you must take in consideration in the next stage of your career.

6.4 Not a ladder

One of the most popular and enduring metaphors for career is the ladder. When we start working, we step up onto the bottom rung of the ladder. Each time we make an advancement, by learning new skills, taking on new responsibilities, earning a pay rise, or gaining a new title, we move up another rung on the ladder. Note that the prevailing theme of this image has to do with 'moving up'. This image of career – that you start at the bottom and make your way up over time – is so embedded in our cultural frameworks, that we don't often question the validity of it. Anything which doesn't fit into this concept is suspect. We have a whole cultural vocabulary around people who don't start at the bottom, for example, think of the concept of 'nepo babies'. Not starting at the bottom and working your way up is both derided and aspired to, depending on the context.

We also have problems describing career moves that don't clearly represent a move 'upward'. We have developed a concept of a 'sideways move', but in many contexts this term is used to soften the blow of a move that is clearly not seen as desirable. Clearly, the goal of a career, as it has been imagined and codified into our culture over the past few generations, is to have a steady upward trajectory. In large organisations, HR departments have finely tuned this upward rise, with each step up the ladder precisely defined and codified. Some businesses try to get rid of this rigidity, perhaps by having flatter leadership structures or by having mechanisms that allow people to 'jump' more fluidly. But the power of the ladder metaphor over our thinking remains.

We have already highlighted that a linear career pattern from education to retirement, reflected in the idea of a ladder, is not compatible with the realities of longer lives or the landscape of work in the 21st century. We hope that future generations adopt a different metaphor and approach to their career, perhaps something with more fluidity, risk, change, fun, something which can embody cyclic changes, learning and meaning. If you are in midlife now, though, you have most likely grown up in a culture obsessed with very rigid concepts of career and success. How can you acknowledge this cultural baggage and explore new ways to think about what success looks like as we age? Let's start by looking at success itself (Exercise 6g).

> **Exercise 6g:**
> How successful do you think you are? Can you list the indicators of success (or no success)?

6.4.1 Career success

Our ideas of success can be objective or subjective. Did you list income as an indicator of success? One might argue that, all else being equal, income should operate as an objective indicator. However, context still applies. Incomes in the legal field may differ radically from those in education. In the global context, the definition of a good salary will vary greatly depending on where you live. And of course, the 'all else being equal' qualifier in the previous sentence, never really applies. We can see this in how often we use language to qualify these measures. We might say 'She is really successful, for a woman' or 'Given his background, he's done rather well for himself'. So, we want to make a point that, even objective measures of success, such as income, have a level of subjectivity. However, more or less objective measures – how much money you make, what your title is, how many Oscars you've won, how many sales you've made, how big your bonus is, how many square feet your house measures, etc., are often used to talk about success and normally rely on comparison against others or set expectations. These kinds of measures work well with the ladder metaphor. So, when you upgrade to a bigger house, you move up a rung; when you downsize, you move down or not, depending on the parameters of success used, for instance children leaving home to their own homes vs. downsizing to save money. The key here is that there is an expected indicator of success, a benchmark.

A subjective measure of success, on the other hand, doesn't lend itself so well to comparison. One such measure might have to do with happiness, fulfilment or personal balance. For instance, Claire was a successful banker with a big house, a fast car, friends in high places, and an ulcer. Now, Claire has downsized. Her house is considerably smaller, she owns a small local business, she has strong ties to her community, and she feels healthy. She still has the fast car, which is both a good investment, and fun. Is she more successful now? This is a subjective measure. In Claire's case, 10 years ago, she would have picked the former as a mark of success; now, she would pick the latter. This is because her priorities have changed, and as a result, her definition of success has changed too. Claire may very well decide to change careers again in the future; her next career move may be back to the fast lane, or it may head off in a different direction altogether. The point is that Claire is deciding, based on her subjective measures, what it means to be successful, and she is open to change. Claire's perception of career has moved away from the ladder metaphor; she sees career as less structured, and more about her personally, from inside out.

This is not to say that the ladder metaphor – and its inherent incentive to keep moving up a rung – is bad. In fact, it may be a useful visualisation of early career progression for most people. It may be a good motivator and help one to make good choices as one is starting out, and well into midlife. At some point, however, the ladder mindset may actually work against us. It could end up blocking opportunities at late career stages. The strategies we employ at early to mid-career are not necessarily effective at the next stretch. So, a sustainable view of career success is more connected with our subjective assessment, personal development and growth than the accumulation of status symbols. This approach to career success is very much echoed by career and longevity experts.

6.4.2 Success or status

One of the problems inherent in changing your measures of success is that the old measures are still alive and operating around us in our social milieu. We attach status to success, and for many people, the loss of (perceived) status can be a barrier to making change. If you are at a stage in life where the ladder mindset is no longer working for you, it can still be hard to let go. How can you get to point where it feels okay to let go of the ladder? What you need to do is to be able to recognise your value and self-worth independently of the ladder. This might mean re-evaluating the importance of status, or at least, of setting your own parameters. How can you do this if you have spent much of your life associating self-worth with how high you can climb? Perhaps the first step is letting go from the pressure of not having achieved x, y or z. Thus, make peace with where your story took you, accepting what did not work for you and acknowledging what you achieved. Let's start with a brief reflection (Exercise 6h).

> **Exercise 6h:**
> Continuing on the topic of career success, reflect on the following questions:
> - How important to you is status? What exactly does that mean?
> - Does the ladder mindset still work for you? If not, can you think of a different way to visualise your next move? If yes, is there any way to prepare yourself for when it no longer works?

An example of this is Fatima who had always dreamed about working for a big consultancy firm. However, a family loss in the final year of university impacted her final grades and consequently her chances of securing a graduate job at any of the main firms she had in mind. Because she didn't get her dream graduate job, she ended up taking a job in a smaller accounting firm local to her. Her boss at the time was developing a boutique approach to his firm, focusing on SMEs willing to pay more to receive good service, but which could not afford the big price tag of the premium firms. Fatima joined at a time of fast growth and ended up progressing to senior level quickly, while developing a particular flair for premium customer service. Fatima now is often approached by headhunters representing different financial and professional service firms. Despite her success, Fatima still resents not having had that big firm experience in her early career. She understands that her 'early career' will never come back, so there is no point in dwelling on the past. Fatima also knows that she will never fully enjoy the career she built, unless she lets go of the sense of failure from missing out on an indicator of success that is no longer relevant.

Fatima is not unique; over the years, we have heard many similar stories of not being accepted to a selective school, or of having to let go of a profession due to qualification equivalence or visa reasons when moving abroad (see Rowson et al., 2022). With all of these, there is one aspect in common – the need to let go of unrealised dreams and unfulfilled ambitions. We are not being negative. While it is good to have dreams and aspirations, it is unhealthy to be trapped by them when they don't materialise. In fact, one of the great secrets of ageing well and living longer and happier lives is the ability to disengage from or forgo things which no longer adds value to our lives, e.g., career aspirations, activities, positions or roles. It is also equally important to celebrate our success and appreciate the good experiences we have along the way.

Another important step in moving away from the ladder model is trying to find an alternative approach to career. Perhaps something akin to the Protean learning cycle proposed by Hall (see Chapter 2), which is a career pattern characterised by multiple cycles of exploration – trial – establishment – mastery – disengagement. Or in more everyday language, cycles of 'been there', 'bought the t-shirt' and 'moved on to something new'. Thus, a Protean career is more about our personal learning journey and our own definitions of success and satisfaction rather than a pre-defined pattern of steps. Of course, in addition to letting go of the ladder mentality, we need to know ourselves well enough to be able to drive these learning cycles. In midlife, we have accumulated enough experiences to make this level of self-awareness and self-knowledge possible (Denyer & Rowson, 2022). We would say it is a sweet spot for a change in paradigm. This approach to career naturally makes us more adaptable, which is an extra bonus when it comes to personal leadership in the age of no retirement.

6.5 The bottom line

In this chapter, we have focused on professional identity. We have explored the idea of professional brand and career-awareness exercises to start unpacking our professional identity, its patterns, drivers, twists and turns. We talked about the concept of success and alternatives to the ladder metaphor. When combined with greater self-awareness, understanding our professional identity helps us to gain a sense of purpose and direction. This doesn't necessarily mean having a 'mission' in life, but gaining a map or compass to understand what works for us and what does not. This allows us to exercise personal leadership, while being true to our agenda and not purely to social expectations. With this sense of purpose in mind, we can start exploring the idea of alignment in the next chapter.

Chapter 7
Identifying your life domains

The previous two chapters were focused on self-awareness and professional identity, which together comprise the first aspect of our personal leadership model: purpose. In this chapter, we will be moving on to the next aspect of our model: alignment (Figure 7.1). Alignment ensures that our actions are consistent with our purpose, keeping our focus on what truly matters. This prevents us from wasting time, energy, and resources on things which no longer matter. This aspect contains two parts: life domains and resources which will be covered in turn in Chapters 7 and 8.

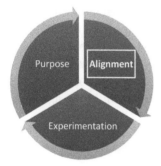

Figure 7.1: Alignment, Sustainable Personal Leadership Model.

Life domains extend beyond the conventional work-life dichotomy, instead these are fluid and personal to each individual. They include roles, identities and priorities which are important to us. Now that we understand our purpose and direction (though self-awareness and professional identity awareness), we are equipped to explore which life domains are most relevant to us, and which are just a distraction.

7.1 This is not about work-life balance

It may seem odd to the reader that a chapter which uses the phrase 'work-life balance' freely and often should start by declaring that 'This is not about work-life balance'. The concept of work-life balance has been used so prolifically in the last few decades that it has become common parlance to talk about one's work-life balance without, we suspect, thinking about the implications of the expression. There is a popular notion of 'work-life balance' which represents these two on a scale, or balance. When working with clients or in our workshops, we spend time disentangling this model of work-life balance (Exercise 7a). What does it mean? What assumptions underlie it? Is it useful?

https://doi.org/10.1515/9783111316147-007

Let's look at some of the many ways in which this concept falls short.

7.1.1 'Work', 'life' and contraposition

The first has to do with the fact that there are only two categories – life and work. This implies that everything is either work or life, and crucially that something cannot be both. Intrinsically we all understand that this distinction is nearly impossible to make. Where is washing the dishes? Is that work or life? Does work mean those things we get paid to do and life is everything else? If so, then what about driving the kids to school, or serving on the board of the local school/church/charity? Furthermore (and more philosophically) isn't all work a part of life? Why should we have a standard model dividing the world into two categories which don't make sense and can't be easily separated from each other? Notice that there are two issues here: one is that there are only two categories, and the other is the labels that we give to these categories.

The second thing that bothers us about this concept is that it is conceived as a balance. A balance is a type of scale in which there are two sides which are weighted against each other. If you add more weight to one side of the scale, that side will lower while at the same time the opposing side will raise, and vice versa. Thus, the two sides are always acting against each other. Anything you do to add to one side of the scale will automatically decrease the other side simply because of the way that a balance works. If we were only talking about time, then this might not be problematic; there are only 24 hours to the day, and any minute spent on one side is a minute not spent on the other. But in fact, this model is used in such a way that it represents more than just time; it's used to think about emotion, energy, satisfaction, etc. The meaning of a balance is that each side acts in opposition to the other; they are inversely proportional.

Let's think about what this means with respect to the 'work-life balance'. Many of us will have had situations where something difficult or stressful happened at work (lowering the scale on the work side) and this then had the effect of lowering the 'life' side of the equation, in contradiction to the model. Let's say that you are having difficulties with a co-worker. This causes you to be stressed and possibly also to have feelings of anger, unhappiness, or some other negative emotion. Does it seem unlikely that these feelings will suddenly disappear when you leave the office? The work-life balance model implies that when you are burdened at work, the life side will be lighter; instead, you find your negative feelings and low mood encroaching on everything else. The negative situation at work 'bleeds' into other aspects of your life, like family time, exercise, etc. On the other hand, let's imagine that you are given a new project at work which is challenging and for which you are receiving positive feedback and notice. You feel engaged, and you have lots of energy. Isn't it likely that this positive feeling will also spread to other things you do, that is, into the 'life' portion of the model? These positive feelings will 'feed' into other aspects of life. We can see from these examples, that 'life' and 'work' do not act in opposition to each other. It is not the case that energy, or time, or emotion expended in one area will always and necessarily be met with the opposite movement in the other area.

7.1.2 Implicit judgements

Another thing we don't like about this work-life balance model is that it is implicitly sexist. This has to do in large part to how the term 'work' is understood in our general cultural perspective as 'paid employment'. The model seems to suggest that everything that happens outside of the office or paid work environment is 'life', thus it implicitly assigns many areas of unpaid work to the 'life' side of the scale. For example, childcare, or managing family life (scheduling, driving, shopping, cooking, cleaning). While it is true that these tasks are perhaps more equitably divided than 20 years ago, it is still the case that the responsibility for many of these more often sits with women. In fact, although these tasks have historically been termed 'women's work', they are generally understood to sit on the 'life' side of the equation. Although not explicitly stated in this way, a quick read of some of the books and articles on work-life balance or popular discussions of it on podcasts, talk shows, etc., shows that the model implicitly assumes sexist definitions of work.

One of the things that we find especially insidious about the model is that it is judgemental. The assumption is that 'balance' is good and 'imbalance' is bad, where balance means that you have reached a point where you can put equal weight or energy or resources into the two sides. Walk past the self-help or business shelves in any bookstore and we are bombarded with instructions on how to reach this balance. Underlying the whole enterprise is a feeling that if you can't reach this perfect balance, then you are failing. Social media amplifies this with Instagram and other photo sharing apps showing us how 'easy' it is to have a work-life balance in which everything is camera ready and picture perfect. This narrative creates a false vision of the ideal worker/mom/dad/spouse, etc.; even if we know that it is likely staged and photoshopped and taken out of context, it is hard to not feel guilt or shame or envy that we can't make everything fit seamlessly. This aspect of the model feels preachy and judgemental and has a 'one-way-fits-all' approach that we suspect leaves many feeling inadequate and unworthy. It suggests that if you haven't got 'balance' then you aren't trying hard enough.

This leads to our next point: that this work-life balance model does not take into account money and personal resources and how this may affect the scale. It feels elitist. When we read books or articles extolling how to achieve a good work-life balance, we often find ourselves thinking 'Well, yes, this would be easy if I only had x', where 'x' can be more money, or better health, or access to flexible work hours or reliable childcare, or maybe a housekeeper to manage the household. Perhaps you've felt this way too? As such, this advice feels at best unhelpful, and at worst, it reinforces our feelings of being stressed and inadequate. We teach workshops in many parts of the world, and our participants have often pointed out that the model feels very Western; it assumes a particular vision of how family and communities are structured. From this perspective, the model can seem both unrealistic but also selfish, as it ignores the additional responsibilities one may have to the extended family and community, and also the societal expectations towards supporting and uplifting others.

7.1.3 Personal balance

Having already established that the work-life balance model is problematic, how can we talk about it? What terminology can we use that doesn't come with its own negative assumptions and judgements? In the discussions that follow, we will use the term 'personal balance' to refer to the sum of all of the different aspects that make up your life, good and bad, energising and depleting, fun and not-so-fun, and of the decisions that you make which result in more time or money or effort being put into one aspect of your life over another. Importantly, 'personal balance' as we will use it, is not conceived as a scale in which work and life are pitted against each other. Nor does it come with implicit judgements attached. Personal balance, in this case, is a holistic measure which reflects where you personally are right now. Your balance is both situational and fluid. It will change as your circumstances change and as the result of decisions that you make. No one but you can judge whether the place you are in now feels right, and no one but you can decide what you might change to make things feel more holistic. Above all, there is no rule book on how personal balance should be experienced, achieved or maintained.

7.2 Life domains and ripple effects

One of the fundamental problems with thinking about 'work-life balance', as discussed here, is that it has too few categories. In fact, our lives are divided into many different 'domains'. Only by digging into which of the domains have meaning for us, and by looking at them individually, can we then begin to build up a picture of how we are utilising our resources and which domains are bringing us satisfaction. For example, instead of trying to lump all of the aspects of your life into either a 'work' label or a 'life' label, you may think about having multiple labels – perhaps one for 'health' and one for 'family and friends' and one for 'volunteering/giving back'. We are going to spend much of the remainder of this chapter working with you on some in-depth thinking about domains and personal balance, but to do that we need you to be able to define those domains which are meaningful to you. We will shortly be introducing an exercise that has you think about 8 distinct domains, but actually the number isn't important; it is a guideline to start you thinking. By defining a domain, what we mean in the first instance is to put a label to it, and to acknowledge that it is an area that you need to consider.

7.2.1 How to choose domains

Let's think about how you might go about selecting these domains. As this is a book about work (a vast simplification but nonetheless a useful descriptor), we expect that one of the domains which you will need to consider is work. Some people might find that a category labelled 'work' is sufficient. Mike, for example, finds it very easy to compartmentalise work; he goes to the office, works a full day, goes home and leaves work behind. For Mike, 'work' is a domain which is easy to define and where the boundaries are clear. Like Mike, Anoop has a clearly defined job that he works at and gets paid for. Anoop, however, is also working a second job; this one is not bringing in any income but it is a project which Anoop is passionate about and which he hopes to develop into an entrepreneurial business in a few years. Faith also has a second job, but this is one that she doesn't have a vested interest in nor is particularly excited about; it is merely a path for her to raise the money for a deposit on a home. It is important to her, and part of her plan for the future, but it has a different kind of place in the scheme of things. In this example, Mike may decide that he has a single domain labelled 'work', Anoop may have two domains 'work' and 'entrepreneurship', and Faith might also have two domains, perhaps labelled 'career' and 'gig work'. The choice of the domains is personal because it is determined by the reality of how your time is spent, but also by the determination of what is important to you.

There are lots of other domains which could be selected. The domain of 'health' is another which is often included, and becomes more important for many as they become older. Again, it may be sufficient to have a single domain labelled 'health' or 'fitness', but some may find it useful to have distinct categories, for example, one for 'physical health' and one for 'mental health'. Sven, who is training for an iron man competition, may have a specific domain for 'training', and Marilyn, who finds she needs a daily run to keep her centred, may have a specific domain for 'running'. We would suggest that some consideration of health, and your health resources (see Chapter 8), should be part of your selection of domains for this exercise.

When considering health factors, don't overlook mental health. You don't need to have a specific category labelled 'mental health' but one or more of your categories could be something that helps you to stay in a good frame of mind and improves your emotional outlook. For example, if drawing or singing makes you happy, you may have a domain for 'art' or 'creativity'. If giving back to the community makes you feel good, then 'volunteering' or 'community' may be a good domain to consider. Margaret, who has a busy career and three active children, picked 'quiet time' as one domain. It was something she wanted to make sure she considered while reflecting on her personal balance and choices.

7.2.2 Domains not chosen

It is also interesting to consider which domains you haven't featured and why. Although we can argue that the choice of domains relevant to personal balance is individual – the absence of certain aspects of life can be detrimental in the long term. Peseschkian and Remmers (2020), in their model of balance for well-being, suggest that our domains should reflect for key aspects of life: (1) biological-physical (e.g., health and fitness), (2) rational-intellectual (e.g., work and achievement), (3) socio-emotional (e.g., family and friends) and (4) imaginative-spiritual/meaning (e.g., purpose, culture) in a dynamic equilibrium. Some domains may fulfil more than one aspect only. For example, Carmen believes her work domain covers rational-intellectual and imaginative aspects. Eric derives both socio-emotional and meaning from his family domain and relationship with his children. Paradoxically, there are moments in our workshops when participants express neglecting one of these aspects, often biological-physical, due to their limited time or energy. For Peseschkian and Remmers (2020), this is not sustainable and it is worth delving a bit more into why and how long this is likely to continue.

7.2.3 Domains over time

Your life domains are part of the mix of your life and we want you to consider each of these things both separately and as a whole to see how they affect your sense of balance, and to consider how your choices can affect this balance. Some domains are more permanent than others, and these may change with time and circumstances. In our example of Faith, who is doing gig work in order to save for a house, that domain has a fixed end; when it stops, her selection of domains will undergo a re-evaluation. When Jabulani begins studying for an Executive MBA degree, he adds 'education' as a domain. Frank was never worried about health until he developed diabetes; now he understands the importance of this domain and also realises that it will have ripple effects into other domains. As a result, he adds 'health' to his list of important domains.

Many things happen to us as we go through the experience of living which change the responsibilities, roles, resources, interests, opportunities, and communities that we have and take part in. This reflects the fact that life domains are both fluid and personal. It is also the case that changes in one domain can impact across multiple domains. For example, if there is a change to your health, it can have ripple effects across many other domains. This is another way in which the domains are fluid; although we think of them as individual domains, they are all connected and it is unrealistic to imagine that change doesn't impact across the system.

7.3 Wheel of life

Let's look at an exercise which is ideally suited to getting you thinking about balance in a more holistic way. You may have seen this before; it is called the 'wheel of life'. The exercise has a circle or wheel which is divided into eight sections. The first step of the Exercise 7b is to label the sections. This is where your thinking on life domains comes into play. Only you can determine which of these domains should be part of your mix, as explained in the previous section. Figure 7.2 is an example for which the user has chosen the eight labels: work, family, fitness, mental health, finance, hobbies, romance, community.

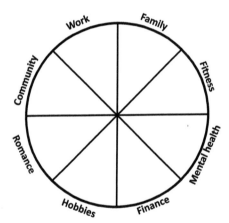

Figure 7.2: Wheel of Life.

Exercise 7b:
Think about the domains which you need to include in your wheel, and label the eight sections.

Once you've labelled your domains, there are several steps to using the exercise, and these have a natural progression to them. The first has to do with satisfaction or happiness. Think about each of these domains independently and for each one, ask yourself 'How satisfied am I with this aspect of my life currently?' Each spoke is divided by lines which are marked from one – near the centre – to ten, at the outside or the rim of the wheel. As you consider each domain, you can colour in the section of the wheel (or piece of the pie, which may be an easier way to visualise the sections) to correspond with your current level of satisfaction, with '1' meaning 'not very satisfied at all' to '10' meaning 'fully satisfied'.

It goes without saying that this is an exercise which demands honesty; it is not helpful to put down the answers which you feel are expected of you (more on expectations later). You are not preparing this so that you can share it on social media. Rather, it is the first step in a deeply reflective exercise. The exercise will lose value if you start out by choosing satisfaction values that are not truly accurate for where you are now. Most people will find that there are some domains where they have high levels of satisfaction and some where they have low levels of satisfaction. If you were to imagine this wheel moving, it would most likely be a very bumpy ride.

Exercise 7c:
Consider each of the sections of your wheel and ask yourself how satisfied you are with that aspect of your life. Shade in that segment accordingly.

Let's consider some examples. Previously we mentioned Jabulani, who has started an Executive MBA degree. Jabulani has picked his 8 domains for the exercise, which include one for the MBA. The degree is a major commitment of time, energy, and money. It is a part-time degree, so it is accomplished alongside his already significant work and family commitments. It was a big decision for him to commit to the three years it would take to complete the programme. In Figure 7.3, we can see how Jabulani has labelled his wheel, and also the degree of satisfaction that he gains from each domain.

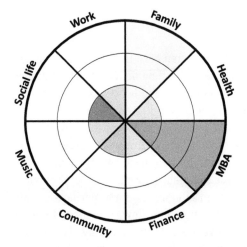

Figure 7.3: Jabulani's wheel, indicating satisfaction.

As you can see, his satisfaction level for the MBA is very high; it is challenging and is both intellectually and socially stimulating. In contrast, his satisfaction level from 'work' is very low. In fact, it is this very dissatisfaction with work which has led Jabulani to choose to do the MBA degree. He feels as if his current work situation does not have an upward trajectory, and he believes that the MBA will give him more options for a successful future career. There is a lot of juggling which he is doing now to fit in the extra study time, and this means that he is not able to spend the time he would like on his health or on his wider commitments to the community. Both health and community are important to him, but these are areas which he is currently paying less attention to in order to manage the MBA. He is unhappy and guilty about the extra weight he is putting on and the fact that he has withdrawn from the board of a community project which he had previously supported.

Louise is on a career fast track. She has had three recent promotions and is now a senior vice president in her organisation, which comes with a good deal of responsibility and autonomy. People respect her. She is involved in mentoring young women through her professional organisation. She is proud of coming so far in such a short time, and she has worked hard to achieve this. Louise has spent years working late into the night and on the weekends. She has a good income and is happy that her financial situation is strong and gives her many opportunities for the future. However, her focus has been on her career advancement for so long that she has ignored other aspects of her life. She rarely spends time with friends or with her nieces and nephews. She is beginning to wonder whether it is time to make adjustments. When Louise draws her wheel, she is very satisfied with career and finance, but much less so with social life and creativity.

7.3.1 Expectations and satisfaction

We are asking you to measure satisfaction, but it is often hard to separate satisfaction from expectations. Are you satisfied with a particular domain, say career, because you meet the expectations of others? Or are you dissatisfied because you don't meet expectations? Perhaps you are happy with one domain but are feeling pressured by others to want more or to change direction. And let's not forget the expectations which we place on ourselves. Sometimes we can be our own worst enemies. We are all too often harder on ourselves than on others; this can mean setting ourselves up for failure and dissatisfaction. Sometimes these self-made expectations were set many years ago, and we may find that we have been clinging to them, perhaps unconsciously, as our circumstances and life paths change and flow. Shouldn't these assumptions and expectations be taken out and re-evaluated periodically? We suggest you return to Exercise 7c now for a reality check – are you unhappy in any of your life domains because you are in the wrong place? Or because you are asking too much of yourself? Or because of others' expectations?

Participants in our workshops often find this exercise very revealing and may use it to make big changes. Martin was a successful banker. He had met every measure of success in his career, particularly financial success. However, he felt as if he had gotten into banking in order to meet other's expectations; he had pursued a high salary because in his circle it was a comparable measure of success. Since becoming an adult, he had invested his energies into 'keeping up with the Joneses.' At the same time, however, Martin could not stop wondering whether he would be happier if he had pursued an earlier dream to be a social worker. The weight of not knowing whether he had made the wrong choice pulled at him and kept him from enjoying his success. Jürgen had a solid fast-track corporate career with all of the perks. But he felt that something was missing. He had an idea to start a small charitable organisation which would work with local governments to support employment opportunities for disadvantaged youths. He worried about what other people would say. Would they think he was throwing away a big salary and guaranteed financial future to pursue a sense of purpose and community?

Part of the appeal of doing an exercise like this (and what makes it hard work) is that it forces you to dig deeper and to try to separate out expectations (both of others and of yourself) from satisfaction or happiness. Both Martin and Jürgen were able to use this wheel of life exercise as a stepping stone for considering whether they were in the right place. Martin stepped back from banking for a while to pursue other options. Three years later, he was back in the banking business, this time without the weight of wondering whether he was in it for himself or for others and was feeling energised and happy with his choices. Jürgen also evaluated expectations and satisfaction and decided to get off the corporate ladder and start his charitable organisation. This move felt right to Jürgen, and that sense of rightness spread outwards into other domains of his life, as a ripple effect.

Of course, it is one thing to identify the expectations which you feel are influencing your choices and your happiness; it is quite another thing to disregard them. It may be worth revisiting the idea of objective vs. subjective success we explored in Chapter 6. Our very notions of success and achievement are often determined in comparison to others – socially, financially, academically, etc. These social comparisons can take a negative spiral and lead to impostor syndrome or perfectionism, both of which can keep us from succeeding or from being happy with our achievements. At its worst, they can affect our mental health. While some social comparison is unavoidable, the detrimental effects can be minimised if we understand the power of expectations in shaping our experiences. These days, social comparisons can be unhealthily amplified on social media channels, and it is a good thing to be aware of so that you can keep things in perspective. Moreover, it is important not to lose sight of our 'inside-out' motives and drivers when it comes to evaluating satisfaction in any of our life domains (see Chapters 5 and 6).

7.3.2 Resource allocation and energy

Now that we have completed this step of the wheel of life exercise by examining each domain with respect to satisfaction level, it is time to do the exercise again from another perspective. This time, instead of looking at satisfaction, we want you to consider the amount of energy or resources (e.g., time, effort, attention) which you are currently investing in each domain (Exercise 7d).

> **Exercise 7d:**
> Draw a new wheel with the same domain labels. Consider each section of your wheel and ask yourself how much energy or resource you invest in that domain. Shade in that segment accordingly.

Once you've completed this for your eight domains, have a look at the wheel as a whole; you should be able to get a good picture about where you are currently investing your resources. Is the picture as you expected? Or perhaps you have discovered that there is a domain which is taking up more resource than you had assumed? Let's say that you have elderly parents whom you care for, and the exercise demonstrates to you in a clear way how much of your resources (time, money, energy, etc.) you are investing in that role. Understanding this may help you to re-direct some resources from some other domain, or to think about how to import resources from elsewhere, for instance by getting help. Another example is Julia, who noticed she was not investing enough time or effort in maintaining her physical fitness; at the same time she was not spending enough time with her children. This was a particular moment in her career when she was time-poor. Looking at this picture, she decided to combine efforts and signed up for family tennis sessions, allowing her to spend some fun time with her children and exercise at the same time. By looking at your wheel of life from this perspective, you may see some interesting patterns emerging about where your efforts, time and resources are being used, and which domains take up most of your attention and focus. Although you may think that you have an implicit understanding of how much you are investing in different domains, it is often the case that previously unacknowledged patterns come to light when looked at in this way.

The wheel exercise, however, becomes much more insightful when you compare the two wheels. By looking across the wheels, you can compare the amount of satisfaction you are deriving from each individual domain with the amount of resources you are committing to it. You can also take a holistic look at the two wheels and perhaps see overarching patterns that may give you insight into your balance. As an example, let's compare the satisfaction and the investment wheels for Jabulani, who we discussed before (Figure 7.4). Recall that Jabulani is dissatisfied with his job and career and so has started an MBA with the hopes of shaking things up. We see here, not surprisingly, that Jabulani is committing a large amount of resources to the MBA, and he is also receiving a great deal of satisfaction from it. Conversely, since so much of his 'spare' time is spent studying, Jabulani is not investing resources into his health and community service, and as a result he is unhappy with each of these.

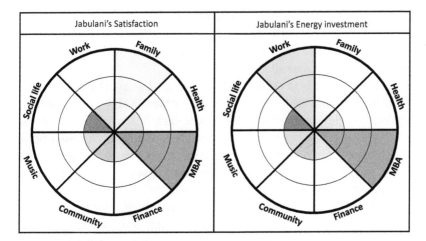

Figure 7.4: Jabulani's wheel, comparing satisfaction vs. energy.

7.3.3 Misalignment and recalibration

The more interesting domains will be those where there is a 'mismatch' between investment committed and satisfaction gained. Jabulani is unhappy with his job, but he still needs the income and it is critical that he is able to retain his post while doing the MBA. He doesn't want to invest the time or the resources in looking for other work until his studies are complete. This means that he sticks with it, investing much more time than he wants into a job which provides little satisfaction. Conversely, the mismatch for family runs the other way. Jabulani gets great satisfaction from his family; they are a supportive, loving unit and he relishes his role as a spouse, father, and son. However, due to the extra demands of the MBA, he is spending far fewer hours with them than he would like. For the moment, this is working, as his family is fully supportive of his efforts. Both mismatches could be the cause of concern and could lead Jabulani to do some reassessment of his personal balance. Looked at as individual domains, however, he finds that he can rationalise each of them: Because he considers the job a (temporary) means to an end, he is willing to stick with it until he completes the MBA. As his family is supportive, he rationalises that he will make up the time with them afterwards, and furthermore, that they will also benefit from his MBA as his income and job prospects should improve down the line.

A different picture emerges when he considers the wheels holistically. While he can justify his investments and satisfaction with each domain individually, as a whole they are more difficult to explain away as a temporary artifact of the MBA. With the exception of his studies, all of the things which bring Jabulani connection and joy are being short-changed. He is spending less time with family, less time with friends, less time with his music, and less time with community engagement. Is it any wonder that his satisfaction levels are low? Also, he can now see how easy it is to ignore those things which keep him centred and boost his mental health. Seen in this way, Jabulani may now wish to re-think how he allocates his efforts.

Another example of this kind of mismatch is Patrick, who has been quite dissatisfied with social aspects of his life, while all other life domains in his wheel felt broadly fine for him. When exploring the level of investment in each domain, he noticed that he was putting a lot of energy into his social life and friendships. This followed a couple of years of neglect, when he was very focused on his career, studies, and his health. Despite his efforts and time, he was not getting anything out of his social life. For him it was 'a lot of partying and superficial friendships'. Up to this point, Patrick did not realise that his approach to his social life was not working for him anymore. Misalignment such as high investment and low satisfaction means either the investment strategy is wrong or the focus (goal) within a domain is not true to who we are. For Patrick this wheel exercise was a wake-up call that it was time to move on from partying, and instead to focus more on meaningful social relationships. Those relationships and social life that also require an emotional investment, beyond any time and money spent. Now, try this comparison yourself (Exercise 7e).

Exercise 7e:
Compare each of the domains across your two wheels, individually.
–   Do you see any misalignments?

Now look at the two wheels holistically, and compare.
–   Are there any patterns that emerge?
–   Do you see places where you need to make a change?

7.4 Evaluating the sustainability of life domains

In the previous sections, we used the wheel of life exercise to examine a chosen selection of life domains by examining them in relation to the satisfaction we derive from them, and the resources we commit to them. In doing so, we considered each domain individually, and also considered the collection of domains holistically. In this section, we would like to extend this exercise one step further by considering the issue of sustainability. We alluded to sustainability when we looked at 'mismatches' between satisfaction and resource commitment; for example, in the case of Jabulani who can rationalise the resource he commits to the MBA because he understands that this commitment has a fixed time period associated with it. Here, however, we are not primarily concerned about mismatches and justifications but about examining each of our domains in terms of its long-term sustainability given anticipated and unanticipated changes in resources. Two resources which have the ability to change quite substantially as we age are health and finance, and changes in these will cause ripple effects over the entire wheel, that is, they will affect multiple life domains.

To begin, have a look at your wheel with its selected life domains and ask yourself 'What is the sustainability of this domain over the next 5 years?' 'Over the next 10 years?' Does your job, for example, require a particular degree of physical strength or dexterity? Is that sustainable over a long period? For example, Mary is a surgeon. The job requires optimal health, dexterity, focus, fine motor control, experience and continued practice, and the ability to make decisions quickly and take responsibility for and leadership of teams of health care professionals. At the age of 40, Mary may well see this domain as very sustainable over a long period of time. However, as she ages, Mary may find that she views this domain as more time-critical; perhaps she worries about decreased dexterity, perhaps she no longer wishes to put in the hours performing surgery that allow her to keep both her skills and her knowledge fresh and sharp. Mary can make decisions about the longer-term sustainability of this domain. Perhaps she envisions retiring, which will allow her to switch up her domains, making others more resource-intensive while she winds down the work domain. For example, she could envision a wheel ten years into the future in which community involvement, volunteering, or travel take the place of career. Alternatively, she may anticipate that there is a time limit to her active surgical career, and begin to direct her professional life into new areas which take advantage of her experience while acknowledging this timeline. For example, she may explore teaching or administration or working for hospital boards. How sustainable is your current wheel of life (Exercise 7f)?

> **Exercise 7f:**
> For each section of your wheel, ask yourself how sustainable you believe this domain to be. Are you likely to have the necessary levels of resources to maintain this domain in 5 years? In 10 years? Considering the wheel as a whole, how sustainable is it?

The discussion of the wheel of life exercise began with some insights into how to choose the domains you would utilise; in short, these domains are personal to you and are important to you for one reason or another. In the context of sustainability, we should also mention that these domains are not permanent. Like all else in life, they are continually in flux. The fact that your domains are subject to both expected and unexpected changes, and that any change may cause ripple effects across the entire system, means that it is important to have a system which has some capacity for resilience. We can connect the idea of sustainability as we've used it here with resilience – if/ when life events happen that require our attention, e.g., health, caring, accidents, redundancy – is there resilience in the system?

One way to build resilience is to manage resources efficiently. Where are your resources optimised and where are they used inefficiently? This will also involve an understanding of your values – which things are most important to you and where do your priorities lie? Are you able to move resources from one area to another when your needs or priorities change? Another way to maintain resilience is keeping an open mind to explore other options. Savickas (2020) refers to concern (about the future), control (over our choices) and curiosity (experimentation) as key factors in finding our next adventure before the current one is unsustainable. Therefore, drawing our wheel of life is not only an exercise for now – it is also an exercise for the future. It is ultimately an exercise of choice within a limited set of possible options.

7.5 The power of being selective

Kooij (2015) defines successful ageing at work as the maintenance of high levels of health, motivation, and work ability among older workers. She utilises the idea of person-environment fit (P-E fit) in which there is a match between the needs and abilities of employees and the requirements of the role. Her work focuses on how workers can actively enhance their P-E fit by regulating their behaviours. Because both the individual employee and the work environment change continually, it takes effort to maintain a good P-E fit. If there is a change which means that the fit between the person and the environment diverges, then the individual may need to regulate their behaviour or seek workplace adjustments if those are available.

We can see how this relates to our discussion of sustainability and resilience. If one of your domains, for example health or finance, changes, it may affect the fit that you have in your work environment, and then you will need to actively make changes in your priorities and behaviours in order to either ensure a better fit or disengage and develop new goals.

Selection, optimisation and compensation (SOC) theory (Baltes & Baltes, 1990) describes a set of strategies and behaviours which enable us to make better choices in our life priorities (e.g., goals, activities, domains) and deploy our resources more efficiently as we grow older. SOC strategies, as the name implies, involve being selective when choosing our goals, activities and roles. This selection can be based on our priorities, wants, aspirations or best returns, i.e., what is most fulfilling or rewarding to us, or contributes most to increasing our resources. This selection can also be loss-based, for example, when we can no longer perform well at something. This loss-based selection tends to happen more frequently later in life, or when going through a particular shock such as to our health or finances or a caring-related responsibility.

Improving our ability to make choices allows us to do more with less, letting us be more focused instead of spreading ourselves too thinly. However, letting go is not an easy task. We can see that when we revisit the wheel of life activity that often we are putting our energy into things that give us little back, or that simply are not needed or expected of us. A good example is when we get promoted or take on a new role at work, letting go of previous tasks and responsibilities can be really hard. Often, we see individuals accumulating more and more activities rather than allowing others to take over, thereby depleting their resources. Being selective is also understanding how much effort to put into our commitments, when to retreat, take a break or bring it to a close. The ability to be selective does not come easily to many of us. It involves saying no and setting boundaries. Social media often elevates unsustainable or false narratives of being able to do it all; if only we could get up early enough and drink enough green smoothies, we wouldn't have to let go of anything. It can be hard to make decisions to ignore these narratives. However, the evidence clearly shows the importance of being selective as we live longer.

Once we have narrowed our field of action, we are then able to drive our resources to improve our experiences. This next behavioural strategy is called 'optimisation'. Which means, for instance, prioritising time and effort in mastering our approach to what we do, in order to improve our performance and/or the quality of our outputs. For example, a marathoner may decide to stop other peripheral physical activities so they can direct their energy and time to improving their running performance. Mary, our surgeon, may choose only to operate in the mornings when she feels the most refreshed, rather than having surgeries booked all day.

The final strategy is called 'compensation'. This comes into play when our resources alone are insufficient to achieve our goals or participate in the activities we choose. Thus, compensation helps us to adapt to changing personal circumstances, life stages, and contexts. In the case of the marathoner, this may mean to continue running but perhaps to switch to 10k runs or to community-based fun runs. In the case of Mary, this may involve switching tasks so that she is more focused on teaching/training, or clinical practice, and less on the physically demanding action of performing a surgery. For someone with a chronic illness, it may mean making a series of compensations, for example, moving to part-time work, or switching roles to one that can be done remotely from home, and changing responsibilities as certain tasks become more difficult. While we may see optimisation more positively than compensation, both types of behaviour are beneficial. They allow us to be engaged in the things that are important for us at a level that does not compromise our sense of worth. The opposite is to stay stuck, trying to make something work when it clearly does not. In fact, it can be very detrimental to our mental health to set ourselves up to fail by insisting on something that we can no longer perform or from which we derive no joy or fulfilment. So, as with anything, a sustainable strategy is about accepting that adjustments are part of the journey (Exercise 7g). Personal leadership is about smart decisions, the ones that gives us the best return on investment.

Exercise 7g:
Reflect on the questions below:
–   Identify areas, activities or goals that you could let go of now or in the near future.
–   Now, identify 1–3 areas, activities or goals which are a priority for you.
–   From one of those, identify how you could optimise it (and, if relevant, compensate)?

7.6 The bottom line

In this chapter, we focused on the first element of alignment: life domains and personal balance. We introduced the idea of personal balance as something personal, fluid and more complex than the dichotomy of work-life leads us to believe. We explored the relationship between expectation, investment (e.g., effort, time, resources) and satisfaction when evaluating our life domains. We also highlighted the need to have a sustainability mindset that allows us to have more choice and control over our future, enabling us to make the most of our increased longevity. The next element of our model delves into our personal resources. This is an artificial separation, as the conversations around life domains and resources are intrinsically linked. Alignment here is more than bringing those two together, but ensuring that what we do is consistent with our purpose.

Chapter 8
Recalibrating your resources

The previous chapter was focused on life domains and personal balance. Here we will explore the second element essential to achieving alignment (Figure 8.1): resources. We will explore the variety of resources that are available to us and the need to recalibrate, maintain and build our reserves. Understanding the dynamics of personal resources we have at our disposal is essential for us to be able to make smart leadership decisions about the roles and contexts in our lives. Aligning our purpose (vision, goals) to our reality (domains, resources) is a powerful way to embrace experimentation, in the form of reflection and action, as we recalibrate and explore new paths from midlife onwards.

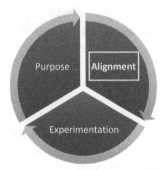

Figure 8.1: Alignment, Sustainable Personal Leadership Model.

8.1 Personal resources

We have been referring to 'resources' in different points of this book and now we will delve into what resources mean in the context of longer lives. The notion of resources is very much the same whether we are talking about organisational, business or personal resources. We define resources as 'advantages we hold which can be used to either further our position of advantage or mitigate disadvantages we encounter or possess.' These advantages can be tangible – like money, education or employment – or less tangible, like confidence, resilience or optimism. Understanding the dynamics of these resources is at the heart of successful midlife transitions and ageing well. It allows us to make the most of our advantages as we get older so we can manage ourselves sustainably.

Much of the literature on resources builds on the research of the psychologist Stevan E. Hobfoll, and his theory named 'conservation of resources' (Hobfoll, 1989). While his work has been geared to understanding stress and trauma, it has been applied to several different areas such as career management, life transitions and suc-

https://doi.org/10.1515/9783111316147-008

cessful ageing. Hobfoll defines resources as 'those objects, personal characteristics, conditions, or energies that are valued by the individual or that serve as a means for attainment of these objects, personal characteristics, conditions, or energies' (Hobfoll, 1989, pp. 516–7). He makes clear that we need these in order to acquire or develop more resources, and that when we are well-resourced, we are more likely to accumulate even more. This is akin to the idea of advantages enabling more advantages and vice versa explored in Chapter 4. The fundamental difference is that resources, according to Hobfoll, are limited. Individuals need to actively obtain, retain, and protect them. Intuitively, we can see this is true, e.g., there is just so much time, money, energy, etc., at our disposal. Low levels of resources may lead to stress and may hinder our ability to respond to different life challenges.

Life circumstances and events have the potential to deplete individuals' resources, threatening their status, position, economic stability, loved ones, fundamental beliefs, or self-esteem. Loss of resources can be significant for us in two ways: Firstly, these hold practical value for individuals, and secondly, they bear symbolic importance by contributing to our sense of self and identity. This is illustrated by the case of Cynthia, who has always been known for being confident and frank in her interactions. At midlife, Cynthia started to struggle with anxiety which impacted her confidence and ability to be open and direct with others as she once was. Very few around Cynthia noticed any change, and she claims she managed to hide it well. Yet, Cynthia didn't recognise herself and found it hard to accept the loss of this resource. Before we continue here, we would like to reassure the reader that this story has a happy ending. Cynthia regained her confidence over time and feels herself again. Confidence here is a psychological resource that was taken for granted until she lost it. Beyond how her day-to-day functioning was affected, confidence was fundamental to her sense of self and 'being confident' was part of her identity. Resourcing herself was essential to be herself again.

Stories like Cynthia's are quite common, and there are many other examples of individuals who depleted their resources. These are not always regained to the same level as before. On a positive note, we can always grow and widen our set of resources, expand our advantages and maintain a healthy stock. This is essential to optimise our midlife and create a sustainable future. Sustainable personal leadership entails managing our reserves, staying attuned to their levels. Managing our resources is a life skill, like swimming. We never know when we will need them, but when we fall in the water, we better have our resources available so we can make our way to shore. This may go beyond our ability to swim, but also having access to floating devices and knowing how and when to rest.

Actively managing our resources inevitably involves recalibration. This includes understanding of our life demands and what are our priorities at present and in the future, such as we explored in the previous chapter. As we already reviewed our life domains, we will dive into the resources that matter in the era of increased longevity.

8.1.1 Personal leadership resources

Definitions of resources, such as Hobfoll's, are open to interpretation. This means that we all have different ideas about our resources. While we agree that the specifics of our resources are individualised, it is useful to have a broad direction of what resource areas are relevant for an engaged retirement. For our sustainable personal leadership model, we are informed both by career development and ageing research (see Chapter 2); therefore we will be combining insights from these two disciplines to define key areas of resources.

We will be building on the career resources framework proposed by Hirschi (2012) – reviewing previous published works, he integrated essential resources for a self-management career approach. Like Hobfoll and the ideas of cumulative advantage (Chapter 2), Hirschi emphasises that developing one resource area can help to develop others. The loss of resources can also have ripple effects and lead to resource depletion in other areas. So, the dynamic of resources is like a spiral – it can spiral up or down. For instance, the lack of knowledge or skills to do a particular job (human capital) is very likely to have a detrimental effect on our confidence (psychological resources) and even impact our work relationships (social), goals and sense of self (identity).

In the case of Cynthia, the loss of confidence led to a threat to her identity and may have also impacted her relationships. Therefore, our resources need constant attention. Other authors within the career domain refer to resources as 'capital' (see Arthur et al., 2005) – despite criticisms of its parallel to financial language, it pretty much reflects the dynamics of resources. The resource areas we will discuss are not presented in any particular order, no one is more important than the other; they are interdependent, as evidenced by the ripple effect and spiral dynamic.

8.2 Human capital resources

This area of resources refers to our skills, knowledge and attributes. These can be achieved through education, experience, training or having access to information. We tend to think of human capital simply in terms of our profession, e.g., 'I am a qualified accountant and have knowledge of accountancy'. Human capital, however, should be a bit broader than occupational specifics, and should also include general work/career/job market skills and knowledge. So, one not only needs to keep up to date with trends, technology, and advances in their field, but also to keep up with how the job market functions. We often meet in our workshops individuals who had fast-moving careers, or who felt that their career progressed due to luck or good sponsors and mentors. Having this kind of good fortune does not mean they did not work hard or did not deserve it. However, when we don't have to carve out opportunities in our careers by ourselves, we don't necessarily acquire the skills and knowledge of how to do it. In the worse-case scenario, we might not even be able to recognise our own strengths and potential.

Many of us feel the need for a change in midlife, maybe because we moved on from certain aspirations, changed our priorities, or because we want to experience something different. Therefore, learning to build our human capital for the next adventure is key for a successful transition. The next adventure might be a continuation from what came before – in which case exploring how to remain relevant and competitive is the goal. Other times, when seeking something new, the task is to recognise the experiences we can leverage and what we may need to develop. Often it is not the availability of opportunities that is the issue, but rather appreciating that we may have more options than we thought by knowing our human capital (HC).

Thus, knowing the current state of our human capital resources is key. As these are always changing, this means re-evaluating them periodically. Then we can examine them in light of our goals and aspirations and develop a learning agenda, to build up and keep fresh those resources which will help guide us forward. This is an iterative cycle – the resources we have will impact on the goals and aspirations we have, and those goals and aspirations will help us to make decisions about which resources to invest in and which to let go. This iteration is what we refer to in the model as recalibration. Note that, although the state of your HC will impact on which directions you take, this does not mean that your goals cannot be big and crazy, or take you in completely new directions. The skills, knowledge, and experience you have should be available to you as you move forward, but should not be seen as necessarily limiting your path. In Chapter 9, we will give you a blueprint for exploring changes through experimentation – both big and small.

We can think of human capital in terms of knowledge, skills, and attributes. **Knowledge** includes, for instance, technical, functional, sectorial, organisational knowledge and gaps. **Skills** involve practical application of knowledge, tacit knowledge, experience, and soft skills. For many of us, distinguishing skills and knowledge can be difficult as some items can appear in either category. If this is the case for you, it is okay to think of these two together. **Attributes** are all other personal qualities that may be relevant, such as values, personality, beliefs, attitudes, traits, abilities and strengths. We generally find in workshops that people tend to be more familiar and comfortable reflecting on their human capital than with other types of resources. This is probably because we are accustomed to listing our knowledge and skills in contexts such as writing our CVs, going to job interviews, introducing ourselves to colleagues, and presenting ourselves professionally.

The point of a CV is to curate your knowledge, skills, work experiences, and attributes in order to secure a particular job opportunity. Thus, a CV is already highly selective. Yujin is a software designer with expertise in systems software for health care. On her CV, she lists all of the jobs she has held that are relevant to this career, as well as her educational achievements, the computer skills that she has, and certain personal attributes, such as being highly focused. She may mention the fact that she is multilingual. However, she is likely to leave off many of her experiences, and knowledge which she feels is not directly relevant. For example, the fact that she has lived in multiple countries and has developed skills in self-reliance and flexibility as a result, as well as emotional resilience. She may leave off the fact that she is an avid gamer. She is also not likely to mention those areas where she lacks experience. She may feel that she struggles to manage a team, but she is unlikely to list it on a CV. Thus, while a CV is a good indicator of your human capital, it is too narrow for the type of resource audit we are suggesting here. This is especially the case if your next adventure is something new.

8.2.1 Auditing your HC resources

Let's think about what an audit of your human resource capital might look like. Imagine that you could list, in a broad and comprehensive way, the skills and knowledge that you have accumulated, for whatever reasons. This would involve thinking about the whole picture, not just those things you would normally draw on in an employment context. It would also involve reflecting on which of those things you enjoy doing, as well as where your expertise lies. While you may be able to sit and make a list like this, it is likely to be easier to do by working backwards; that is, by thinking about your goals and aspirations and then making as comprehensive a list as possible of all of the skills and knowledge you have that you may draw on to meet a particular goal. Included in this approach would be to acknowledge gaps – what kinds of skills would you need to develop in order to move in the direction of this goal? In this sense, an HC audit is not just about understanding the set of your transferable skills and knowledge, it is about thinking about how to actively build on the set that you have in order to move in a new direction (or to allow yourself to stay comfortably on the path you are on by keeping up to date professionally).

Let's look at Yujin again. She is at a point where she is not feeling challenged in her work. She could move companies, or take on more responsibilities where she is, but she would really like to do something different. She has been thinking about trying to find work in the video gaming industry as a games designer. Yujin has done some research and she knows that she has many of the skills necessary – an IT degree, experience in coding, etc. She also has an understanding of user experience from being an avid gamer herself. However, she could use more direct experience with graphics and other aspects of coding for the industry. After doing an audit of her human capital, she decides that she should pursue a graduate certificate in game design to add to her already strong set of skills.

Let's look at another example. Tebello is just starting her MBA and the process of going back into education has caused her to think more deeply about her career. The first step of this process is to have a goal or outcome to be the focus of her audit. It is okay if at this point the goal or outcome is tentative or exploratory. In Tebello's case, she is exploring her readiness to move to a leadership position. As part of exploring her human capital resources, Tebello not only engaged in reflection by herself, but also asked friends and work colleagues to help her identify any blind spots – good or bad. She notes that she has a wide set of useful knowledge and skills to help her take on a more strategic role. She knows her industry well, has a good understanding of finance and project management and good people skills. She also notes that she struggles with decision making, especially under time pressure or in ambiguous contexts. She decides to work with an executive coach to try to understand her issues around decision making and to see if she can develop strategies to mitigate her stress. She also explores ways in which she can use her MBA to specifically target other areas – such as increasing her influencing skills and also gaining a better knowledge of strategy.

Now, let's explore an extreme example of HC audit which happened during a workshop Kelly delivered. Luiz, the participant, who worked as a human resources director, started his HC audit based on a goal to set up an ecotourism helicopter tour company in South America. Luiz listed the skills and knowledge he would need to develop: He would need to learn to pilot, get a helicopter license, learn about different South American countries' environments and tourism industries, find out more about eco-tourism, etc. Luiz' idea was astonishingly pie-in-the-sky, given that he didn't have any of the expected skills or knowledge necessary to make this happen. Yet, by creatively brainstorming all possible ideas with other workshop participants, thinking about how to move all of the various pieces together, having aspirational long-term plans, he was able to get to the heart of the matter: He was bored and wanted to pursue something grand and exciting. Luiz was able to identify intermediate steps that could be taken to do something along the lines of his crazy idea, like researching the business landscape of ecotourism and his possible transferable skills. He also reflected on how he could indulge his need for change and adventure that emerged during this exercise, by bringing a bit of this to his life even if not professionally.

These different examples involved making active decisions to expand one's set of HC resources. Sometimes, your decision might be to stop investing in maintaining certain HC resources. For example, Mikka is a licensed and practicing critical care nurse. As such, he is required to keep up his skills and current best practice by engaging in a fixed number of hours of continuing professional development (CPD) each year. When Mikka is presented with an opportunity to join a start-up with a colleague, he jumps at the chance. However, he meticulously keeps up his CPD as a critical care nurse, so that he has a fall-back plan, in case the start-up is unsuccessful or unfulfilling. At some point, Mikka will face the decision of whether to abandon this CPD. He may decide to do so for a variety of reasons. He may find that he is no longer feeling healthy enough for that type of high-stress environment, or he may find that he is enjoying his new path and has no wish to return. In any case, he will be making a decision to decrease his HC resources in a way that will limit his ability to make certain choices in the future. This kind of letting go is a common occurrence as we age and our resources and interests and circumstances change. Letting go doesn't have to be negative; it can be very freeing. Is there a good fit between your HC resources and your goals and aspirations (Exercise 8a)?

Exercise 8a:
Think about your goals and aspirations for the next 5–10 years, however crazy or conservative these may be.

Now, in a broad and comprehensive way list all the skills and knowledge that you have accumulated. Consider the whole picture, not just those things which you would normally draw on in an employment context. This would also involve reflecting on which of those things you enjoy doing, as well as where your expertise lies.

Finally, consider also the areas you could learn more about, whether they are completely new things or perhaps an update on what you already know.

Making an audit of our human capital resources is very informative, and can allow us to challenge our beliefs about ourselves. Very often this is a positive exercise. It helps us to move away from an all-or-nothing mindset, allowing us instead to appreciate that we may have areas to address but we also have accumulated resources. It gives us the materials to do a better gap analysis. In the workshops we run and in our coaching sessions, we find that individuals are able to identify ways forward on the HC and contemplate options that may previously have been too intimidating. At a minimum, it provides us a good picture of how resourced we are in terms of human capital – and what else we should be learning and developing to help us to stay relevant in an ever-changing world and work environment.

8.3 Social resources

This area refers to our social relationships, networks and connections, and to the benefits we obtain from our social relations in the form of information, influence and solidarity. Unlike other resources, social capital differs because its source lies outside of the individual. Social resources can be instrumental for us to successfully cope with positive or challenging transitions in our lives. Others can support us to achieve career success faster, find our feet as we move into new roles, or be more resilient in the face of difficult life changes and transitions.

That said, many people feel unsure about how to build and utilise their social resources. They may be unsure of how to find a mentor, use mentoring, nurture or expand a network of contacts, or other concerns. There are several strategies and techniques to fully utilise our social resources. Often these involve lists or mind maps with names, some annotations on the quality of our relationships with those named, as well as any gaps. Typical categories are friends, mentors and sponsors, managers/bosses, clients, colleagues, mentees, other professional and personal connections. To create a full network, mapping should involve our 'hot' network – the people we know well, but it should also consider our 'tepid' and 'cold' network – e.g., acquaintances and friends of friends. This kind of exercise can be a bit overwhelming for someone who has never given much thought to their social resources.

A good way to start engaging with our networks of support is to set up a 'personal board of directors'. This means a group of people who take on specific roles to support us in different or complementary ways just like the board members of a company. For example: we may have someone who is good at coaching us, someone else who is good at encouraging, counselling or giving us feedback. We may also have collaborators, connectors, mentors and or sponsors. We can also identify where there are social capital gaps; that is, roles or functions which are not filled, or are under-filled. We may need to invest some time and effort to find someone who can fit appropriately into these gaps. Some of these roles are informal or emerge organically, but in certain circumstances we should explicitly agree or formalise the nature of relationship and support we are seeking. For example: What role would a given board member like to play and how this would work (e.g., monthly meetings, ad hoc calls, etc.)?

As you recall, in Chapter 1, we introduced the idea of you as the CEO of Self, Inc., making leadership decisions about how you set goals, make strategies, and allocate resources to improve the health and well-being of yourself. If we carry this metaphor forward, it would make sense that Self, Inc. would have a board of directors whose role it is to give advice and support to the CEO. This relationship involves trust and honesty, and also allows the CEO to draw on expertise.

In our workshops, it is not unusual for someone to express feeling uncomfortable with the idea of benefitting from their social networks. However, it is key to remember that when we leverage our social resources, we are building meaningful relationships with others. We are also humanising ourselves to others by normalising the idea of seeking and receiving support. Still, it is important to acknowledge the support our personal board members give us when we achieve our milestones or overcome barriers. This is whether they were voluntarily supporting you or were someone you hired (e.g., executive coach). A hand-written thank you note, acknowledgement on LinkedIn or even a little celebration can mean a lot.

The idea of a personal board may not capture the other side of our social relationships, such as our mentees, supervisees, etc. So, we would like here to make a point that leveraging our social resources, is not simply 'taking' but it is also 'giving back'. When we develop others, we are also developing our leadership capabilities, thus gaining a whole new range of skills. In midlife, supporting others is particularly relevant as it also coincides with a phase of life in which we are naturally seeking to help others and make our mark through generativity (see psychosocial development in Chapter 2). Therefore, in addition to our personal board, we should also think about on whose board we would like to participate.

If we take the example of Tebello we explored before, she identified some areas of human capital resource development needed for her to progress successfully to a leadership position. She also identified that she might benefit from working with a coach. Examining her social resources a bit deeper, Tebello realises that although she has many friends and a loving family who are great cheerleaders, her personal board is missing individuals who could play a key role in supporting her personal leadership development and career progression. Having a sponsor and/or mentor is important for her as she is looking into moving to a different level of the organisation. They can help her to gain insights into how she is coming across, what works in the organisation and also to secure support when decisions about promotions are made. Given that Tebello is a well-liked person and very sociable, she doesn't think it will be an issue to complete her personal board and took note of a few names she will be approaching soon.

In the case of Luiz, working with a career coach he identified the need to find mentors – other individuals who had made radical career changes or are experienced in the 'adventure' type of businesses. As his ideas become more tangible, he would certainly need other roles to be filled, such as 'connectors' that could help him expand his network in a new sector. Luiz would also need to choose his 'cheerleaders' very carefully; to make such a drastic career change he really needs some ruthless compassion and not simply someone that would be applauding his moves without a critical perspective. So, for Luiz a personal board is a way to de-risk his career moves but also ensure he is not drifting or lost along the way. Exercise 8b gives you the chance to examine your social resources.

Exercise 8b:
Reflect on the status of your social resources:
- Who are your personal boardroom members and what roles do they play?
- Are any roles missing or in need of being filled, given your current needs or future plans?
- Are you involved in giving back (belonging to someone's personal board)?
- What actions should you be taking to have an effective personal board?

Note that our social resources are dynamic; the roles which are critical to us at any one time may fluctuate as our circumstances change, and the people who fill those roles will also change. This is why we should consider keeping the flames alive in different parts of our network and light up those connections when needed. The actions to keep these flames alive range from being aware of our network, to reaching out to our connections from time to time. As a rule, our network will only support, help or recommend us if they have us in mind. And this only happens if we make ourselves visible (beyond posting on LinkedIn). This visibility, however, is not about projecting our well-crafted, social media selves. It is acting with integrity and honesty, aligned with who we are – thus, bringing our inside-out professional brand to the fore so we are true to ourselves. The same 'visibility' principle applies whether you are seeking or offering support to others.

8.4 Psychological resources

This area refers to the internal and mental attributes or qualities we possess which contribute to our overall well-being, resilience, and ability to cope with life's challenges. These resources play a crucial role in our ability to be flexible, adapt, and cope with life's changing demands – thus, they play a role in our mental health and stress response. However, we don't necessarily feel psychologically resourced equally across all our life domains, and it is not unusual to find people who are very positive about their professional lives (highly resourced) and feel less positive about their personal domain (poorly resourced), or vice versa. This is because this area of resources is internal and largely subject to our interpretation of events. This element of subjectivity makes psychological resources significantly more malleable. Therefore, it can be effectively strengthened by interventions, as well as depleted or derailed because of cumulative or discrete events, for example in the case of trauma (discrete, disruptive), or microaggressions (cumulative and less visible). Perhaps this is why many authors allude to the fine line between the need for therapeutic or non-therapeutic interventions to address imbalances or gaps in psychological resources. We echo this caution, and believe it is important to emphasise that in certain cases talking therapies are the best approach to restoring and strengthening one's psychological resources.

When non-therapeutic interventions are appropriate, executive coaching, personal development workshops and even self-reflection can be extremely effective. Amongst the many approaches to understanding and developing psychological capital, we will be using the PsyCap model developed by management professor Fred Luthans (Luthans et al., 2007). The ideas around PsyCap emerged with the positive psychology movement, which is focused on stimulating optimum functioning and thriving rather than treating pathologies. There is plenty of scientific evidence supporting its effectiveness enhancing overall psychological well-being and performance. PsyCap includes four basic internal resources known as 'HERO': Hope, (self) Efficacy, Resilience and Optimism – these resources overlap with a range of other psychological resources found in the literature (e.g., self-efficacy links with confidence). Like psychological resources more broadly, PsyCap is malleable. Understanding how this model works can help us to use these resources better, as well as how to improve it. In Figure 8.2 is a simplified explanation of the PsyCap's four internal resources 'HERO'.

Although these are treated as separate resources, they overlap and influence one another. If we are optimistic in how we frame or attribute explanations to what happens to us, naturally we will be more resilient. If we are more resilient, we will probably feel confident we can complete our tasks or overcome challenges successfully (efficacy). Likewise, if we have other PsyCap resources, we are likely to feel we have enough agency to set future goals and lead ourselves towards them. So, when it comes to PsyCap, and psychological resources more broadly, it is like a spiral that can go up or down. Of course, here we are most interested in how to promote and facilitate an upwards spiral. To improve some of these internal resources we may need to take

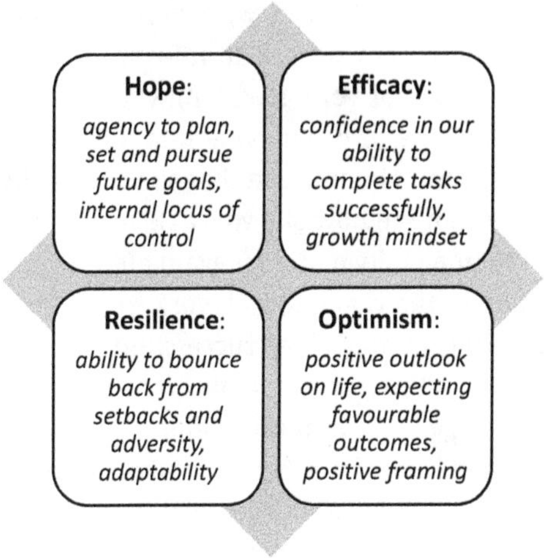

Hope:	Efficacy:
agency to plan, set and pursue future goals, internal locus of control	confidence in our ability to complete tasks successfully, growth mindset
Resilience:	Optimism:
ability to bounce back from setbacks and adversity, adaptability	positive outlook on life, expecting favourable outcomes, positive framing

Figure 8.2: PsyCap's HERO adapted by the authors.

actions to build up other career resources, such as developing our skills (human capital) to improve our efficacy, or finding a mentor (social resources) to boost our hope or optimism. Before we give some examples, we suggest you pause to reflect on your PsyCap (Exercise 8c).

Exercise 8c:
Using the PsyCap HERO model, reflect on your psychological resources' levels.
- Do I have goals and aspirations that motivate me? Can I see myself achieving these goals or getting out of difficult situations?
- Am I confident I can accomplish tasks, achieve goals or overcome challenges even in light of unexpected events?
- How do I deal with stress, pressure, or unexpected changes in my life or work? Am I easily discouraged? Can I learn and become stronger from adversity?
- How do I interpret failures and setbacks? How defining are these negative events? Looking ahead, do I expect a lot of good things for me in the future?

You may also like to consider:
- Examples of when you successfully demonstrated these resources
- Other possible explanations or frames to evaluate previous experiences
- Possible strategies to boost your hope, (self) efficacy, resilience or optimism
- PsyCap in different life domains, e.g., home, love life, career

8.4.1 PsyCap in action

Some of these resources can be improved by simply reframing our experiences, thus finding an alternative (more positive) interpretation or focus to events in our lives.

This is very much linked to the idea of our personal narratives we covered in Chapter 5, but zoomed in to specific scenarios or instances we use to inform our self-evaluations. For instance, Miriam often says she is not very good with change. This broad belief about herself is now getting in the way of her moving into a different division of her company. Working with her mentor, she realised that she is actually very good with change. Upon examination, she can see how she was able to adapt to moves around the country, first when going to university and then again after getting married. She also adjusted well to having a family and remaining at work.

By finding specific examples where she adjusted to change successfully, Miriam increased her sense of self-efficacy. She would still prefer to remain in her comfort zone, but she appreciates that she can do change very well (and often learnt a lot from it). If we were mentoring Miriam, we would now help her to think of what or who could support her to manage change better if she takes the opportunity ahead of her. Using the evidence of our PsyCap to adjust the framing we use can be extremely helpful in and of itself; but it gains in strength if we take the next step towards identifying strategies to facilitate us achieving what we set ourselves to do.

Another example is Yujin who, as we discussed earlier, is looking into working in the video gaming industry as a games designer. When this idea initially occurred to her, the first thought in her mind was that she could not make such a move. She did not think she would be able to deliver the same competent level of work she currently does in IT (efficacy) or be resilient enough to cope with the lows and downs that are inherent to any transition (resilience). After reviewing her human capital, she realised she was just a few steps away from becoming a good professional in this area. By considering another qualification to add to her HC resources, she was able to counter her lack of confidence in her skills and knowledge. Yujin realised that she could build her competence levels required to succeed in this new area.

In terms of her resilience, like Miriam, she was able to look in her past for evidence that she is resilient and able to cope with challenges as they are presented. For Yujin, however, this reframing was not enough. She decided to set up strategies to ensure her resilience. Yujin recruited a trusted 'counsellor, mentor and cheerleader' for her personal board who would help her to keep on track during difficult times. She also realised that it is important for her to maintain her personal balance through activities that allow her to relax and reenergise. So, Yujin protected time in her diary for exercise, meditation and play. Yujin feels that she has a good plan to maintain her resilience and feels she will be in a good place to overcome all challenges ahead.

Both Miriam and Yujin go beyond evaluating their current levels of PsyCap resources. They also start exploring possible ways to improve them, either through possible actions (e.g., upskilling, seeking more positive and healthier environments) or simply by looking back, reframing experiences, or recognising that we have these resources and have utilised them before. Both strategies are useful, especially as we enter periods of change and transitions, such as midlife.

Psychological resources are not only essential in times of transition and change, they are also essential to maintain our optimum functioning while protecting our mental health from the negativity we are constantly exposed to in the media and social media. We are not saying that we should stay happy and positive all the time, as positivity can be as toxic as negativity when it prevents us from getting in touch with what is really going on with us. However, when we have healthy levels of psychological resources, we are better able to navigate our lives. We encourage you to explore possible ways you can improve your psychological resources.

8.5 Identity resources

While some of the literature combines identity and psychological resources, we take the approach from Hirschi (2012) of treating these as separate areas given their richness. This area of resources refers to clarity around our self-concept, purpose and goals. Here there is some hierarchy; it is difficult to define and achieve our goals without first knowing 'who are we' and our 'whys'. When we refer to goals, we imply these are meaningful goals that can bring us fulfilment. These are qualitatively different from a 'to do' list or externally influenced goals – but instead informed by a clear sense of self.

Having clarity over our self-concept doesn't mean having a fixed and permanent conception of ourselves. Quite the contrary, it means engaging with who we are, understanding that we change over time, learning from our experiences, and adapting to different environments. Despite our instinctive desire for certainty, our identity is malleable. We are constantly re-evaluating who we are whether we are conscious of it or not. The fact that we are always changing can be quite an empowering thought because it implies opportunities for new experiences. We explored self-concept and purpose in Chapters 5 and 6. To capture where you are now, we suggest returning to your notes and reflections from these two chapters and recording a summary of your insights into a short statement as outlined in Exercise 8d.

Exercise 8d:
Write a short statement introducing yourself.
– You may like to include your values, your preferences, your personality
– And your professional brand

Practice an 'elevator pitch', introducing yourself in a 2-minute speech, while capturing important aspects of who you are personally and professionally.

While self-concept, awareness and clarity are central to this resource area, with an understanding that we are constantly evolving, knowing our goals is also part of it. This entails having a vision for ourselves, a desirable future and goals that are more defined. It also involves having a set of goals that are coherent with each other and coherent with our internalised assumptions. Therefore, knowing our goals, even tentatively so, can give us a head start in our journey towards our next adventure. There is no need to read this book to work out that having a particular target makes pursuing it a lot easier. Anyone who is actively engaged in the workforce understands the principles of setting up an action plan to achieve a certain target. Because, ultimately, goals, big or small, can drive actions as we will see when we discuss experimentation.

Nevertheless, we acknowledge that sometimes we embark on a transition without any idea of direction or goals. That is okay; sometimes we may need to first find the 'what' (and maybe the 'why') – before moving on to more specific actions. How can we develop our ability to explore possible, ideal futures, which can help us to generate goals? We will build on the principles of 'intentional change' (Boyatiz, 2006), namely, that creating a vision of an ideal future is the first step to achieving a sense of direction. In our workshops we often ask our participants what they would be doing now (or next) if money were no object. There is always someone to point out this is never the case; yet we ask them to leave this crucial point out of the equation for the sake of exploration. Just as with a brainstorming session or a child's play, we encourage our participants to engage with this hypothetical question around an ideal scenario. The timeline of this question is an individual choice – 'now' for the ones who already feel the need for a change – 5, 10 or x years from now for the ones who are starting to think about the changes that may be needed sometime in the future.

Remember Luiz, who was considering the helicopter eco-tourism business in South America? We pointed out before that this was a very pie-in-the-sky ambition given the current state of Luiz' human capital resources; that is, Luiz didn't have much of the knowledge and skills that he would need to run such a business. Upon examination, we can also see that this goal might turn up in an exercise like this one; Luiz doesn't have the financial resources available to do this either. However, this is probably the case with most start-ups – the idea, the spark, the belief, often come before the financial wherewithal. The clarity of the goal does relate to Luiz' identity resources. Luiz knows what he wants to be doing. Having this clear insight into his goals will help to guide Luiz into decisions, and may even make up for his initial lack of HR capital to support the goal. He may not yet know how to pilot a helicopter, but his clear focus on the goal will help him to allocate resources so that he can develop the skills he needs. His impassioned sense of direction and purpose may help him to recruit others to the plan, those with skill sets that can complement his own.

So, we would like you to try out this thought experiment as well – remember to keep the money factor out of this Exercise 8e, and let your imagination go wild now. We will leave it to you to add the appropriate time scale.

Exercise 8e:
If money is no object, what would you like to be doing (now/sometime in the future)?
–   You may like to describe where you are, who you are with and what you are wearing.
–   What aspects of yourself is at play there, e.g., personality, values, talents.
–   Give as much detail as possible using all your senses.

Now, that you have completed these two reflective exercises, you should take note of your insights; these may lead you to possible areas of exploration and experimentation. We will be returning to these notes in Chapter 9.

8.6 Health and well-being

In addition to the categories of resources derived from the academic literature on careers, we have added health and well-being as things that are key to a sustainable longer life. The importance of this resource area is evident in the literature on ageing well. The role of health and well-being goes beyond having a longer working life as described by De Vos and colleagues (2020) on sustainable careers in Chapter 2. This is about having a good quality of life in general, and feeling fit to make choices that bring us meaning and fulfilment. Because when our health resources are depleted (e.g., due to chronic stress, burnout, physical health) it is very difficult to keep up with other resource areas – and be able to do the things we want. Discussions around mental health, and acknowledgement of the importance of mental health to our well-being, may feel new and uncomfortable in some contexts. There have been stigmas and barriers in place that mean that we don't always consider our mental health when looking at the whole picture – these are steadily breaking down, but can still be hard to overcome in many cultural contexts. However, it is clear that health is a holistic concept – we need to consider the whole body and mind to have a true picture of how we are doing.

Antonella, for example, has rheumatoid arthritis. At its worst, it greatly influences her ability to work. She has had to make adjustments to her role, to the types of tasks she is able to carry out, and to her schedules. She has found that stress greatly affects the disease, as well as her general state of health. When she is anxious, or when she hasn't slept well, for instance, her symptoms may get worse. Antonella knows that to manage her disease properly, she needs to take good care of herself. She needs to get enough sleep and not over-task herself. She practices meditation which helps her feel calmer and more balanced. As an autoimmune disorder, the disease is subject to flare-ups; it can go into remission for periods of time, during which Antonella may be tempted to push herself. She may wish to work over-time to finish a big job, or to go out dancing with friends. Experience has taught her, however, that balance and maintenance are super critical. Her mental state and her physical state are connected and she must take care of both in order to function at optimum levels and decrease the severity of flare-ups.

There is no magic bullet to improve our health and well-being. Most interventions will require some level of lifestyle changes, therefore our commitment and willpower. It does help to start by being honest with ourselves when examining where we stand. We put a list of health and well-being related items for your self-evaluation in Exercise 8f. This is not a scientific list, but some ideas based on what usually comes up in our coaching conversations and workshops discussions.

> **Exercise 8f:**
> **Reflect on areas that are important to you related to health and well-being. Make a list of these areas. For each item on your list,** make a note of how well you are doing. Do you need to make any changes to your habits and routine? How will these changes assist you in optimising your health and well-being?
> Here are some examples of things you may wish to include on your list:
> - Enough/good quality sleep
> - Drinking enough water
> - Eating balanced and regular meals
> - Physically active, exercise
> - Breaks from sitting down
> - Fitness status
> - Energy levels (vs. fatigue and tiredness)
> - Substance intake
> - Overall mood
> - Down time for relaxation
> - Personal balance

You can include different items to this list that are true to you, or consider any chronic condition (e.g., high blood pressure, cholesterol) that you may be managing now. The aim here is to identify what could do with a change – either because you are not okay or because you know your current level is unsustainable. It should also give you some insight into how urgently you need to take some action, how easily these can be addressed, and where you may need some extra help or more information. This exercise is the beginning of an action plan. Remember that even a small, positive lifestyle adjustment can contribute to our overall quality of life; improve this resource area and influence others through ripple effects.

8.7 A note on financial resources and planning

We cannot talk about sustainable futures without at least mentioning the importance of understanding and learning how to manage our personal finance. We acknowledge that not every issue can be solved through financial planning and foresight, and that not everything is under your control. However, exercising more control over our finances enables us to make more informed decisions and helps us to achieve greater freedom of choice in midlife and beyond. We will steer away from any advice or guidance here. We are not personal finance advisors, and if you try to search on Google 'financial planning books retir*' for example – you may find, like we did, that there is already a wealth of information out there (no pun intended). Our search generated about 262,000,000 results (in 0.52 seconds) – which is an indicator that there may be something there for everyone.

We would like, however, to bring to your attention some interesting findings from research on the economics of ageing (see World Economic Forum, 2024). Firstly, people tend to not be very good at understanding what our financial needs will be in the future. We tend to be bad at forecasting how much we need to save, and how long we are going to live. We are also not very good in anticipating what our life circumstances will be, usually basing our judgement on our current reality, for instance assuming our health, fitness, quality of professional network, ambitions, etc., will remain unchanged. Given our tendency to miss the mark here, it is essential that we take a more critical view of our estimates, as well as seek expert advice to help our planning.

The second point is around creating a habit of talking openly about finances. In many cultures, it is difficult to talk about money, as if it were somewhat a dirty topic, something to be embarrassed about. This creates a big problem for couples and families to set a coordinated approach to spending and saving. As social scientists we understand the symbolism of money for many of us, sometimes money signifies power, self-esteem, masculinity or even love. However, when it comes to longer lives, money and finance are essential elements, a practicality that we cannot avoid (whether this is sooner or later). Reframing the meaning of these conversations may be a good way to start feeling more comfortable with the idea of talking about it at home.

Finally, not all of us will be in the same situation in midlife. Some people will be distinctively worse off than others. Here we are not talking about the differences between unskilled, skilled or knowledge economy workers. Within the same category of workers, great disparities can be observed. For instance, divorced individuals tend to be worse off financially often due to division of assets. Women also tend to have smaller pension or savings pots, with some facing late-life poverty. This disadvantage is sometimes linked to gaps in employment (e.g., maternity leave), other times due to systemic discrimination and gender pay gap. So, understanding your risks is an incredibly important part of your planning. Remember that midlife is not too late to start organising your financial resources.

8.8 The bottom line

In this chapter we looked at personal resources. Together with life domains, covered in Chapter 7, these make up the second part of our personal leadership model – alignment. We discussed a number of different types of resources – human capital, social, psychological, identity, health, and financial resources. Each of these are interconnected, to the degree that changes in one resource area can affect other areas, and they are each important to the overall picture. Our ability to examine our resources honestly, and to realise when we need to make adjustments to them as our circumstances change, is part of the process of alignment and of recalibration in general. It is important that we are able to combine making hard decisions with self-compassion; remember that the goal of personal leadership is to provide for sustainable well-being. In the next chapter we will be looking at the third stage of the model, experimentation.

Chapter 9
Experimentation

The previous two chapters were focused on the two elements of alignment: life domains and resources. Together with purpose, alignment equips us to explore possibilities ahead by giving us a direction, setting the priorities and clarifying the resources we have to make it happen. However, we cannot discover new opportunities or commit to a plan without opening ourselves to trying. Just like in scientific studies, we cannot make informed choices without sampling and evaluating if the next step is right for us or not. The need to try new things out makes the last aspect of our model: Experimentation (Figure 9.1).

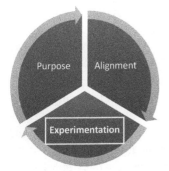

Figure 9.1: Experimentation, Sustainable Personal Leadership Model.

In this chapter we will combine the two elements of experimentation: action and reflection. These two processes go hand-in-hand in our model. Action is 'doing' or 'trying out' with curiosity and openness to learn more about ourselves and the options we have. Reflection is not an afterthought when it comes to personal leadership, but should happen before, during and after all actions. By presenting these two together, we are making an explicit point that an experiment must include both doing and thinking to be really effective and sustainable.

9.1 The case for intentional experimentation

We have been making explicit that shifting our personal narratives can bring positive changes to our lives. When we edit our narratives, in effect, we are re-constructing our self-concept and identity. As we explored in previous chapters, these identity constructions and re-constructions are a natural aspect of life, as we are exposed to different experiences, relationships, roles and learnings. As our self-concept evolves, so do our behaviours, habits, appearance, etc., as these internal and external processes are very interconnected. The other way around is also true: When we start changing

https://doi.org/10.1515/9783111316147-009

what we do, what we look like, the people we connect with, etc. – we inevitably start changing who we are in the world. Snow and Anderson's (1992, p. 1348) seminal work explained that there are a 'range of activities individuals engage in to create, present, and sustain personal identities that are congruent with and supportive of the self-concept which they referred to as identity work'.

The process this construction is experienced through is 'talk and action' (Watson 2008, p. 130) and involves active experimentation and self-reflection (Ibarra 1999; 2007). It includes the use of props and strategies such as selecting and crafting physical surroundings, personal appearance, selectively engaging with social groups, and verbally expressing and affirming one's identity. Therefore, all these strategies are areas open to be tested.

We all may know someone who has 'reinvented' themselves, something that may sound either exhilarating or terrifying to you. However, we want to diffuse the myth that radical life transformations are a product of one major experiment. This is very unlikely. We argue that, when we look closely enough, we can see that in nearly every case there was a series of smaller complementary experiments. These may have been deliberately coordinated and directed to a particular goal. So, our point here is that you may start small and take incremental steps as you feel more confident. This is like learning to ski, to feel the snow and take it from there. Ibarra, who researched major, radical role transitions, summarises the whole journey of experimentation in three broad stages: exploration of possible selves, provisional trials and integration. Although simple, this process can be emotionally demanding (Ybema, et al. 2009), partially because there are no guarantees and because there may be a lot of uncertainty and tentative steps along the way. This is why action and reflection need to take place in parallel. We will elaborate how to prepare for experimentation. Also, instead of exercises, we will be using several examples from our research and teaching practice to illustrate our points and encourage you to think about your own possible experiments.

9.2 Experimentation map

Firstly, understanding what to expect is of immense help in allowing us to feel in control (even if this is an imaginary control). This has to do with our most primitive survival instinct and how we go about associating unknown situations with threat. Embarking on a transition without any awareness of what it entails can be disorientating, leaving us feeling vulnerable and prone to emotional distress. In other words, when we can identify and name what is happening to us and the stage we are at in the process, we are more likely to feel at ease and be more resilient and open to embrace the ups and downs the process will bring. Understanding transitions does not resolve the issues or provide the answers, but it does give us tacit knowledge to plan actions and responses to emerging situations. Here the idea of planning is not having a fixed set of steps, but being prepared and ready for whatever comes up.

A good example is something both of us (Kelly and Tatiana) experienced moving abroad several times. The first time is the hardest, as there is no blueprint or starting point: how to find the good hospitals, schools, nice shops, where to exercise and more importantly our social groups, friends, hobbies and work. Often, when we move for the first time we never even considered where we fit or not, because it had previously came naturally. When approaching a similar change for the second or third time, it is like riding a bike. We know where to start, e.g., beyond the school playground, Tatiana looks for the yoga groups, Kelly the knitting community. We know the things we like or not, how to search for reliable information and how to integrate with others and build a routine. Clearly, every location will have its own characteristics and the 'what' will be different, but the 'how' is very similar. More than that, after a few moves, we know we will be fine and there is comfort and psychological safety in that, which helps us navigate the process.

Similar to our own personal examples is the story of Marilee. When Marilee moved across the country to take up her first big role, she realised that she had a chance to re-define herself. She had spent years in graduate school and working in coffee shops and other laid-back settings. Her wardrobe consisted almost entirely of tee shirts and jeans. When she moved to a new city where no one knew her, she threw out her student wardrobe and invested in a few pieces of good professional tailoring, and some excellent accessories. Her new wardrobe made her feel like a new person and gave her enough confidence to pretend that she was confident. Eventually it worked and she was no longer pretending.

When Marilee moved a second time, she decided to re-define herself again. This time she determined that she would put her hand up for everything; she would become the go-to person on her team, unafraid to put herself out there and be visible. When Marilee made a third move, some years down the road, she evaluated and decided that her previous attempt at re-definition worked too well – she was overworked and overcommitted and stressed out. This time, she decides to be more strategic and selective about when to say yes and when to say no. Marilee realised that, by experimenting with different ways of behaving, she has actually learned more about herself than she might have had she stayed in one place. After a few iterations, she has found a place where she is feeling comfortable in her own skin and authentic. She has avoided being typecast. Marilee mentors young women in her field, and she encourages them to not be afraid of moving, and to take advantage of a move to adopt new styles of being and doing in order to learn what works best for them as individuals.

We can clearly see from Marilee's story that her experiments were never quite the same, but how she approached them followed a fairly regular pattern. Broadly speaking, Marilee starts by reflecting on her priorities and goals, she takes intentional action and reflects on the results. Over time she developed her personal approach to these transitions, thus learning from each and every experience. We can assume that she also became increasingly confident in her ability to drive change for herself. This doesn't mean she did not have setbacks or bumps along the way, but she trusts the process of experimentation when she knows the direction is right.

Learning from experience is the best – but not the only – approach to experimentation. We can leverage the experience of others or read books like this one to create a broad blueprint for navigating transitions successfully. Regular reflection is at the heart of mapping what strategies work for us. In our model, this reflection starts right from the beginning. By this stage in the model, you should have a few pointers to guide your starting point (purpose and alignment). By the end of this chapter, you will have an idea of the process and how others do it through the many examples we will explore. Therefore, whatever your previous experience, you must be intentional in creating a broad experimentation plan leveraging your resources, and don't forget to include space for reflection and evaluation.

9.3 Voluntary vs. forced experiments

This second condition is whether we choose to explore our options or are forced to do so, such as in the case of ill health or redundancy. Very much like having prior tacit knowledge, being forced to explore other options can play on the same mental processes of psychological safety. This is because it takes away our sense of certainty – even though certainty is always illusory. Forced experimentations may also trigger negative feelings, such as rejection, unfairness and helplessness. These feelings are not only demoralising, but they also drain our psychological resources. Choosing to start experimenting puts us in a stronger position to manage the process better.

An example is Jonathan and how he overcame his inertia before having his hand forced by ill health. Jonathan is out of shape. He has a desk job and works long hours. He is also studying part-time in the evenings. His diet isn't great, and his doctor tells him he is pre-diabetic. He knows he needs to do something. Jonathan is also lonely. He puts so much time and effort into work and study that he has let his social life slide. Feeling out of shape and unhealthy doesn't help his confidence in making new social ties. He decides to kill two birds with one stone, so to speak, and to join a group that does some kind of exercise. He considers dancing – just no – and football – really no, before joining a weekend walking group. It is casual and sociable. He gets to talk with new people, get some exercise, and feel less lonely. Jonathan is now planning to take a walking holiday next year, and never imagined he would exercise for fun.

Not all cases are like Jonathan's – whose health concern was a wake-up call for him to try to change and re-write his personal narrative from the sedentary and unhealthy guy to someone who enjoys exercising. In some situations, it can be tricky to control external changes. In fact, it is highly unlikely that we will be able to see it coming every time. Even when the signs are there, we do not always consciously register what is happening. This is something we often see when discussing the topic of retirement with people, or in the case of divorce, or redundancy, or caring responsibilities. Some can rationally see the time to move on or make a change is fast approaching, yet they feel unable to start experimenting with possible options. One participant once said, 'If I start trying other activities, suddenly this will become real'. We understand that experimenting when we are not ready can exacerbate the sense of loss. Because, when we embrace something new, there is always something that we are having to let go of.

Our rule of thumb is to never stop being curious and continuously seek ways to explore new possibilities and experiences, changes big or small. Keeping our curiosity and readiness to act alive, maintains our ability to lead ourselves. Savickas (2020) calls that adaptability. Like a muscle, if we keep it fit and strong it will be there for us when we need it. If we don't use it, we lose it. That loss of readiness and imagination can also deplete our psychological resources, for example efficacy (confidence), and contribute to a negative spiral.

9.4 Experimentation as 'work' or 'play'

In the past decades, there has been a growing academic interest in understanding the nuances of identity construction processes, including how we approach exploration, experimentation and commitment to new selves. Experimentation can be approached as 'play' or 'work' – and very much like voluntary vs. forced changes, these two approaches will impact how we manage ourselves in the process. Ibarra and Petriglieri (2010) propose that play differs from work in terms of purpose, process and place. The purpose of identity play is reinvention and discovery; this is intrinsically motivated and reflects the idea of doing something for fun. Imagine having access to an unlimited wardrobe; play is about trying on funny hats or jackets to see how it goes, how it feels, without any obligation to commit to wearing these items.

An interesting illustration of accidental 'play' experimentation is the story of Philip. He works in a very conservative industry. He shows up for work every day in a navy suit, a white shirt, and a conservative tie. He dresses exactly the same as everyone else in the workplace. He hates the uniform. He feels that as soon as he puts on the dreaded navy suit, his personality and individuality leak out of him. One day, Philip is late for work. He has to rush to catch his train and can't find any clean navy socks. In desperation, he grabs a pair of bright red socks and puts them on. Later that day, he notices a number of co-workers making glances at his socks. They look up at him and smile. Philip is amazed; he has broken an unspoken dress code and life has gone on. The next day, he shows up in a pair of yellow socks, and the day after that, with a pair of lavishly striped ones. Philip continues to wear the same conservative navy suits, white shirts and boring ties every day, but he mixes them up with a vivid pair of socks. Though no one ever mentions it, he notices his co-workers look forward every day to checking out his socks; which pair will he wear today? In an industry where conservatism rules, Philip has taken one small step to expressing his personality, while not overstepping any boundaries. Therefore, if tomorrow he returns to his conservative socks or decides not to commit to that particular act of self-expression it should be fine. Philip is not at any point under pressure to be the 'colourful socks man'.

A further example can be seen in the case of Meg and Eloise, who, quite to the surprise of each, started a podcast. The two have been best friends since they met in their first week of university. They both studied business and management. Meg went to work for a small local firm in Oxfordshire where she worked her way up to general manager. The firm employs 40 people. She lives a few miles from the office and rides her bike to work. The salary is not great, but she likes the people, has good benefits, and low levels of stress. Eloise got hired right out of university by the London offices of a large international consulting firm that employs 6,000 people locally and 80,000 globally. She is now a senior project manager. She works super long hours, earns a good salary plus a bonus if she can bring in projects on time, and gets to travel. The job is hectic and demanding. When they get together, Meg and Eloise spend hours comparing their jobs. Which has the best benefits? Which is more supportive of their development? Which is more fun? Which is more inclusive?

One day, Meg's husband jokingly remarked 'You two should start a podcast.' They laughed it off, but the idea stuck. Last year, they cautiously produced a dozen episodes of their podcast – 'Big firm/Small firm'. It was just a bit of fun at first, but they discovered that they had some insights and that there were people out there who wanted to listen. It was fun and interesting. Surprisingly, they both benefitted professionally from the podcast, which garnered them recognition at work and in the community. They also interviewed other professional women for their podcasts, which helped them to expand their professional and social networks. Although the podcast has impacted on their professional identity, the experiment started out in the realm of identity play.

Unlike play, the process of identity work is externally driven and aims to comply with or achieve an expected identity. This does not mean we that haven't chosen a particular identity for ourselves, but instead that we are committed to shape a particular identity by the end of the process. For instance, when we are promoted to a more senior position, we will attempt to develop our 'manager self' or 'more senior self' even if we are still unsure of what the result will be. So, if we use the wardrobe metaphor again, it is like knowing that we have to choose from a particular section of the wardrobe, e.g., formal business attire, rock-and-roll, sport wear, cowboy, etc. Within these we can then choose what best fits with who we are, and who we are becoming.

A contrasting experience from Philip's 'playful' experimentation, and from that of Meg and Eloise, is the case of Haruto. Haruto is very career-focused. He has moved cities to take up a job in one of the big consulting firms, where he advises clients in his specialty area, intellectual property rights. He does an audit of his resources and realises that he is under-resourced in his professional networks, particularly in this new city. This gap becomes apparent when comparing to others in his firm, so visibility and professional standing are expectations that accompany his position and are essential for career progression. Haruto has had membership for a number of years in a national professional organisation for intellectual property rights, and he has even once been to the annual conference, but at the time, he kept mostly in the background rather than actively participating. Haruto doesn't feel that networking events match his style; he is shy and not good at small talk, but he enjoys working with small groups of people, especially towards a shared goal. He decides that the best way to make connections in the field, and also expand his social base, is to volunteer to be more active in the professional organisation and in its local chapter. Being active in the group is fun and gives him a platform to bounce ideas off of others with similar interests. His expertise is in the growth area of copyright law in generative AI, and he submits a proposal for a workshop at the next annual meeting. Haruto found that making this small change – from belonging to a professional organisation to actively participating in the organisation – has helped him to expand his social and professional networks.

Haruto has taken a different approach to experimenting than that taken by Philip, or by Meg and Eloise. We are not advocating one approach over the other. In fact, it is important that we think about play and work as a continuum and not an either/or approach. Understanding both concepts – identity play and identity work – can help us to make the most of these experiments, enabling us to manage the process better, accept constraints and seize opportunities. Sometimes we will have the opportunity to play, other times it is very much work. In the case of Meg and Eloise, what starts out as play soon becomes much more like work. It depends on the circumstances we find ourselves in, the moment and whether the need for recalibration is inevitable or just an idea. Role changes, like promotion, new jobs, parenting, romantic relationships, or new hobbies all require us to put some effort into finding our own version of the role in question. This is very different from curiosity-driven open exploration, as happened accidentally with Philip. This distinction of purpose affects how individuals approach each process: Play focuses on experimentation and generating diverse possibilities, while work is goal-oriented, striving for continuous improvement toward a predefined ideal.

These two processes also happen in different temporal spaces and places. Identity work is grounded in reality, in present identities, which in turn makes the process more systematic, without much space for randomness or variation. Identity play happens between fantasy and reality. The diversity of experiences is an expected part of the discovery of a possible future self that is as yet unknown. This distinction is really important. When individuals leave work because they are unhappy with their career choice (e.g., leave an organisation job, a particular career) without a vague plan or destination, fantasy and reality collide (see Denyer & Rowson, 2022). This is because it is difficult to be highly exploratory when the pressure to earn a living is pressing.

True play requires a good level of psychological safety; the need for an income makes this safety impossible. So, the time to be completely playful is when life is stable, when we don't have the need to come up with an answer. However, it is not unusual for us to use a combination of play and work experiments in times of transitions. Like a game of chess, understanding the aims, gains and constraints of each approach is key for us to use them in our development.

9.5 Type of experiments

Scientific investigations come in many shapes and forms. This is not different when we are talking about experimenting as part of personal leadership recalibration. We can undertake a thought experiment, a visualisation, a lab-based trial or real-world experiments. All these different types of exploration will have their own advantages and disadvantages which we need to consider in relation to our resources and realities.

9.5.1 Thought experiments

Thought experiments and visualisations are probably the safest type of exploration, because they happen in our minds and imagination which is a contained context. Often this approach is used when the goal is 'identity play', but it is not unusual for executive coaches, counsellors and talking therapy professionals to use this kind of strategy to help their clients to set compelling goals. This is especially the case when the destination is still unclear but the desire to change is real and strong. This is largely because our brains are not very good at distinguishing reality from imagination, and these mental explorations can give us a good indication whether our options are doable or not. Boyatiz (2006), exploring the idea of intentional change, suggests that by exploring our ideal futures in our heads we can elaborate the steps needed to make it happen. Moreover, doing this stimulates a 'feel good' positivity which is essential to open our cognition to generate creative and innovative options.

In Chapter 8 we discussed a reflective question predicated on the assumption 'if money is no object'. Here we will introduce another technique, the miracle question, which is phrased like this: *Imagine that tonight, while you sleep, a miracle happens and you are living your best life (or are doing the perfect job, feeling fit, healthy, happy, fulfilled). However, because the miracle happens while you're asleep, you don't know it has happened. When you wake up tomorrow morning, what will be different that will tell you the miracle has occurred? What will you notice that will let you know things have changed for the better?* Despite any difficulties to keep our sceptical selves at bay, these pie-in-the-sky questions can be extremely effective to help us to locate resources, strengths and refine our self-direction. Therefore, it is a powerful tool of personal leadership.

Juha's experience very much reflects this type of thought experiment. He is a partner in a fast-growing law firm. Despite considering himself quite a resilient person, Juha has been finding it difficult to sleep and recently has been told his stress levels may be also affecting his blood pressure and cholesterol levels. Except for the sleeping issues, Juha does not feel stressed. So, he decided to learn meditation techniques to quiet his mind at bedtime. In the first lesson, the instructor encouraged the group to visualise in as much detail as possible their ideal future, like they are watching themselves on a movie screen (for Juha this ideal future means sleeping well and not having to deal with other emerging health issues). Juha could see himself with an evening routine that allows him to disconnect and wind down, arriving home, catching up with the last emails, taking his dog for a walk and making this as a ritual to a quiet evening with a book. This mental exercise made Juha realise he suffered from FOMO (fear of missing out) which led him to adopt poor work-life boundaries. Of course, sometimes his position required him to respond to issues out of hours, but these were exceptional circumstances and he could always be reached out on his phone. Yet, being 'always on' had become a habit.

This initial visualisation triggered Juha to explore the issue further and consider different scenarios to change his routine. He is now ready to move from thinking to doing, so trying out his options in real life. This story illustrates how thought experiments can be a fairly safe strategy to try. Given the potential benefits, it is hard to justify not using them in the process of recalibration. These explorations come very naturally for some of us, not so much for others. In every case, they can prepare us mentally to try things in real life experiments.

9.5.2 Lab and field experiments

We just made a point about the advantages of using our imagination to explore alternative futures and possible actions. While the upsides are indisputable, these are not perfect replacements for real experiments. This is because with a real experiment, we can have a fully embodied experience of how our ideas, possible identities and options may pan out. These embodied experiments can range from fully 'lab-based', in the form of role-plays (e.g., when we practice a sales pitch in a workshop, rehearse with someone a difficult conversation or try a different approach to presentations), to field experiments (e.g., in the real context of the experiment work, family, leisure activities or in a proxy context like in an interest group, a course, during volunteering).

Frank, for example, was taking a leadership workshop in which role-play was used. The discussion concerned how to engage in difficult conversations. The participants were grouped into pairs and asked to play out a scenario where one of them is an HR director in a firm which is facing redundancies, and the other is an employee who is being made redundant. Frank was extremely uncomfortable with this scenario, and felt that he badly bungled his first attempt to be the HR director. While watching other participants act out this scenario, Frank was struck with the ability of fellow participant Zandile to manage this conversation with a mix of empathy and practicality. Upon questioning, Zandile revealed that she had been in the position on two separate occasions of making large numbers of redundancies in companies where she worked. Frank tried out the role-play scenario again a few times, while Zandile and others watched and provided feedback. He found that with a bit of practice, he was able to feel more comfortable with taking on this role. Frank would never want to be in Zandile's shoes where these types of conversations were a big part of her role, but nonetheless, he recognised the importance of role-play in developing skills, addressing underlying fears and expanding his comfort zone. At work, even though he wasn't put in this exact position, he found that he was able to transfer the skills he learned in this role-play exercise to other situations, for example when resolving conflicts in his team.

Lab-based role-plays, as in the example of Frank above, allow us a safe space to practice in. There is whole field of psychology and therapy dedicated to these trials – psychodrama, gestalt, personal construct psychology, etc. They can be used in the classroom, in therapy or in coaching contexts, among other places. These types of experimentation are safe because they take place in controlled environments, and because there are no real-life consequences. Note that these should be undertaken with qualified facilitators and in an environment where trust and confidentiality have been established. They also allow for iteration, that is, the role-play can be performed multiple times, so that different types of approaches can be explored. Note in the case described above, the importance of feedback and reflection to the process. Frank is unhappy with his first attempt, but he engages in conversation and reflection and then tries again. He is able to do this until he feels more confident. One of the main advantages of the lab-based experiment is this ability to iterate without consequence. Lab experiments are an excellent way to get us confident to try out in real life.

Field experiments are the next level. These take place not in a practice situation, as with the lab experiments, but rather in real life. As such, they may be seen as riskier, but in fact they will fall on a risk continuum, with many experiments still perceived as reasonably safe. For example, proxy field experiences – experiments away from our usual routine (such as volunteering, a club, something for 'fun') can be seen as less risky as there are no major implications if the experiment doesn't pan out. So, although they may necessitate an investment of time and sometimes money, they will be psychologically safer.

As an example, let's consider the case of Liv. Liv has always been shy. She never puts her hand up in meetings and prefers to keep in the background. Liv had a few occasions in school where she tried to speak up and became tongue-tied. Although no one was rude to her, she felt uncomfortable and became even quieter. Nonetheless, she was a brilliant scholar and did very well at university and, despite feeling awkward and shy at job interviews, she has a good record of being highly proficient and results driven at work. However, Liv is starting to notice that more outspoken colleagues are being promoted faster than she is, even with her good record. Once a colleague took credit for her work and she didn't speak up to contradict them. She wants to be able to speak her mind without feeling awkward, but years of habit have made this difficult.

Liv has a few good friends from childhood and with them, she is open and comfortable, and is known for having a wicked sense of humour. One night, while speaking with her friends about her shyness, they challenge her to join an open mic night at a stand-up comedy show. She is in equal parts intrigued and terrified. After some thought, Liv realises that this may be a low-risk way to confront some of her fears about public speaking. Her friends promise to be in the audience and provide support (and laugh at her jokes). No one from work is likely to be there; thus, although there may be some personal risk of being embarrassed and potentially flopping, there are no professional consequences to her career. She can stand up and pretend that she isn't shy. Although Liv found her first open mic night to be embarrassing and challenging, she got up and did it again the next month, and after a few times at the microphone, she felt more comfortable and began to loosen up and let her real self – the creative, funny, intuitive, smart self – shine through. Liv can see the results at work. She was recently asked to make a pitch to a client, something she had always avoided. It has not been an instant change, but having taken one risk and lived through it, she is more open to taking other risks.

Another case of a real-life experiment which slightly increases risk, while still remaining reasonably safe, is that of Klaus. He thinks he is ready to make a step up in the leadership structure of his organisation, but is struggling with impostor syndrome and still in the process of gaining the necessary skills and experience. He would like to experiment with a role that has more leadership responsibilities but would like to do so in a relatively controlled fashion, where he could step back down without significant consequences. Klaus applies for, and attains, a maternity cover position for a colleague. The temporary nature of the post gives him a sense of psychological safety while still allowing him to experience a new level of managerial responsibility. Because he is not expected to make strategic changes in the role, but rather to carry it out effectively until his colleague returns, he can step up and practice applying new skills.

Let's now fast forward 8 months for Klaus and imagine he has done really well and has been offered an opportunity to take a permanent managerial role, in a different division of the company or in a new organisation. This time it would include strategic decisions. If he says yes, the experiments he will need to try as part of shaping his 'managerial and leadership style' start to become a lot higher stakes. This kind of situation happens every day, everywhere, when circumstances change and we are faced with the challenge to perform well in a completely new role. As big believers of 'nothing ventured, nothing gained' we think no chance to develop should be declined – if this aligns with what we want, who we are or are in the process of becoming. However, even very risky experiments can be 'derisked' with the right level of resources and support. Klaus could set up his personal board, or at least identify a mentor to help him with this transition. He can also further develop his knowledge or skills by undertaking an MBA. So, despite the risks – a real-life field experiment is a tangible opportunity to succeed.

9.6 Liminality

While experimentation is an undisputable strategy for sustainable personal leadership and recalibration for engaged retirement, it is not necessarily an instant fix. Especially when it comes to find new adventures, occupations and communities. Often, it takes time to come together and the road may be bumpy and lonely; and as we mentioned before these may require psychological and material investment. Researchers on role and identity transition refers to 'liminal period' as the stage in between letting go of the previous identity – e.g., when we realise it doesn't work for us anymore or is not sustainable – and committing to a new identity. George and colleagues (2021) go further to suggest that the liminal period of major role change – such as a new career or occupation, retirement, parenting – involves more than just identity redefinitions but also requires physical, relational, and behavioural role-related changes. All these elements will dynamically interact, influencing the process of identity transformation and the broad transition experience. Therefore, this in-between period, liminality, can be destabilising. This can be especially the case when we have a 'destination' rather than 'journey' mindset. Transitions are slow, and even the best experiments only partially address the shift needed. Understanding that increases our resilience, enabling us to persevere or move on to the next possible trial.

A good example of this is Pablo. He has been working in civil engineering for his whole life. He had a very successful career and holds a C-suite role. Pablo can sense that retirement, as a bridge employment or occupation, is fast approaching. He knows he should start exploring different possibilities. Pablo always has been good with people; this is largely why he was so successful as a manager. Following a colleague's suggestion Pablo enrolled in a coaching training course. He loved it, and actually met many other participants just like him. Practicing 'being the coach' with the guidance of the course tutors felt safe and satisfying. In the workshops, Pablo could show a side of himself he never had space for in his day job. Before the final workshop, all participants were encouraged to accumulate some coaching hours, so they could discuss their experiences and who they were 'becoming as a coach' in their 'coaching practice supervision session'. When that session came around it was a welcomed space for Pablo to discuss his experience. During the session he recounted that he arranged to meet a coachee late one afternoon in a café in the centre of Madrid. He was coming straight from work and was wearing a suit and tie. Pablo noticed that the coachee was taken aback by his formal attire. He managed to break the ice, but could not help feeling that his wardrobe also should be part of his experimentation. The formal attire was a contrast to the warmth and openness he was intending to foster.

Like many others who are experimenting with spaces, activities and identities very different from their former identity, Pablo kept discovering things that needed to be tweaked and changed. Luckily for him and due to the supportive nature of the course he was taking, Pablo could understand that 'becoming a coach' was a journey rather than a quick fix. This 'process mindset' helped him not to feel like a failure. Pablo is exploring this space in between being a C-suite executive and a coach, but he is not sure if coaching is the next occupation for him yet. Nevertheless, Pablo places an immense value in this experience as a way to get him out of his comfort zone. Going through this coaching course should help him to feel equipped to manage his transition out of the organisation, however that may occur.

Similar to Pablo is the story of Mallory. She has enjoyed a successful career as a civil servant. At 60, she is at an age where many of her colleagues are thinking about retiring. By contrast, Mallory imagines that she would like to be working for another ten years or so, and is eager to stretch herself. Mallory enjoys her job, but would like to explore some other options. She reads about a scheme to take late career workers and retrain them as teachers. This is intriguing and it meshes with her wish to give back to the community. The programme involves a year of higher education classes to qualify as a teacher along with a short internship, after which she is put right into the classroom teaching civics and history to 16-year-olds. Mallory was thrilled to be back in a classroom as a student, and she loved being surrounded by other curious people with similar interests. She found herself debating for hours with fellow classmates, who were often much younger than she was. She enjoyed their fresh perspectives, and also felt that she had a lot to contribute to discussions based on her lived experience. When she was studying, it was easy to get into the flow and suddenly find she'd been at it for hours without becoming distracted. She discovered that the experience of studying as an older adult was so different from when she went to university as a young woman. 'Education is truly wasted on the young,' she thought to herself.

Sadly, however, Mallory disliked teaching teenagers. It certainly didn't live up to her expectations; she found it to be enervating and unrewarding. She put in a good effort, but it didn't give her the spark that the year of studying had. She stuck with it for a year and realised that her heart wasn't in it. Furthermore, she knew that there was no reason for her to keep trying; she was old enough to recognise that teaching wasn't going to suddenly become joyful, and also that there was no reason to continue to do something that she didn't enjoy.

While the 'teaching experiment' didn't work out, Mallory did discover that being a student was very fulfilling. She decided to take on a further experiment, and enrolled as a Ph.D. student. She took up a part-time job doing consulting for charitable organisations, and began an exciting and engaging Ph.D. course. Mallory is sometimes asked 'Aren't you too old to be doing a Ph.D.? What do you expect to gain from it at this point?' For Mallory, the ability to pursue something that she finds so creative and intellectually stimulating is rewarding in and of itself. Of course, Mallory understands that she is in a privileged position to be able to pursue this path. While she does have a pension from her civil service job, she needs to make readjustments to her expectations to undertake this degree. The part-time consulting, combined with conscious downsizing and careful financial planning help to make this possible.

Stories like Pablo's and Mallory's show that sometimes an experiment does not lead to the expected destination. Understanding that this is part of this in-between period helps us not to give up before finding our new identity. There are several beliefs, frames, and thinking errors that may become a barrier and the longer the time frame needed for a successful transition, the more we should be prepared and resourced for this time 'in between'. Having a good starting point, as our model suggests, is a great start. Accepting that reaching a commitment to a new identity may take longer, require more experiments or more attempts than we expected, is also very important. Being vigilant to the signs that we are sabotaging ourselves is paramount.

9.6.1 Barriers to change

Kegan and his colleague Lisa Lahey (see Kegan & Lahey, 2009), when exploring why people struggle to make changes, found that often hidden or unconscious barriers rooted in deeply held beliefs, assumptions, or fears prevented their success. According to them, even when individuals logically understand the need for change, for example taking a particular medication or having a better sleep routine, they would resist (or forget). The incompatibility between what the change means in relation to individuals' hidden assumptions hinders its success. For example, if taking a medication daily means Jane is 'past it' and in decline and she sees this as something negative, Jane may 'forget' to take her pills. Or if Bilal believes that high achievers never sleep and are always on, trying to introduce a better sleep routine may mean to him that he does not have what it takes to be a leader. Unless Jane and Bilal reconcile these hidden assumptions with the changes they want to make, they will never succeed. We argue that understanding our personal narratives can be an effective strategy to identify and challenge these biases. This process includes reviewing our story, as well as examining how our meanings and perceptions are formed and shaped over time. Attitudes, perspectives or limiting beliefs exert an immense influence in our decisions, choices, and ability to take action. Yet, these can remain undetected as we go about our daily lives.

Common thinking errors can also impact the benefits of experimentation. These include overgeneralisation or black-and-white thinking, fortune telling and catastrophising. These errors tend to distort our experiences in a way that we end up with extreme possible options, none of them ideal. We may then seek closure and resolution before we are ready to settle on something new. This means we may end up committing to something that is not quite right, or return to an old self, despite it no longer being relevant or sustainable. Therefore, these thinking distortions during times of transition and uncertainty can hinder our exploration process and prevent us from identifying alternative possibilities that may not have been obvious at first.

Thinking errors can also have implications to how we embark on a change. This nearly happened with Jake, who works for a digital marketing company. He is smart and efficient and has good people skills, and has been moving up in the company at a quick pace. He earns a good salary, lives in an interesting city, and has good friends. However, Jake can't stop his persistent doubts about his work. He is increasingly bothered by the culture of consumerism and is feeling that the work he does for his clients is not aligning well with his personal values. He wants to quit and do something more 'worthwhile', that is, more aligned with what he feels is important, but at the same time he is worried that quitting would be a stupid move. He is honing his skills and developing a good reputation in his field, and his work is respected. One night, over a glass or two of wine, he confesses all this to a friend. Should he quit or should he stay? The friend replies, 'Why must it be all or nothing, Jake? Is there no middle ground?'

Suddenly, his dilemma does not seem so black and white. Maybe he can do both. Perhaps he can stay with his organisation, developing his skills and moving up to a position where he can be choosier about his clients, and let's face it, earn a great salary. Meanwhile, he can volunteer for a cause that he cares about. Jake decides to take on some volunteering – running the digital marketing campaign for a charitable environmental organisation. His skills make a tangible difference to the fundraising and educational efforts of the charity, and he feels great satisfaction at using his talents this way. He realises that this compromise may not always work, but at least for now, he is managing to quiet the niggling voice in his head, and feel good about his work and his contributions outside of work. He is also making connections in the community of non-profits that he may find useful down the road if he decides to make a big change. Having his friend point out his thinking error – of imagining everything from an either/or perspective – has allowed Jake to come up with a better solution.

We highly encourage the idea of utilising an external perspective to help us to see potential blind spots, especially in times of transition and change. This is because a good friend, mentor, coach or a personal board are in a position that is objective enough to identify our potential thinking errors. However, our trusted others are not the only way we can gain more insights on ourselves. Reflective practice techniques are a powerful way to improve our thinking and personal leadership.

9.7 Reflection

There is a well-known quote from Confucius that says that there are three methods to learn wisdom: through imitation which is easiest, experience which is the bitterest, or reflection which is the noblest. In reality, we need all of these processes for our personal leadership development. For instance, we need observation or experimentation to connect with the issue at hand, and to have a reference point. Likewise, we need reflection to make sense of our experiences and observations so we can draw meaning from them. As we unfolded the different aspects of our personal leadership model, we encouraged self-exploration and reflection. We suggested activities and examples to help you to look into your inner world, past and present, to understand your realities and truths. In the simplest terms, reflection means gaining awareness of how and why we think, feel or behave in a certain way so we can make conscious decisions on how to continue (see Jones, 2020). This reflective practice allows us to notice what is going on, separate facts, feelings and thoughts, identify assumptions and bias and have greater clarity about what is going on around us. The process of setting goals, specific or broad, and experimenting with possible recalibration scenarios also includes reflecting on a possible future (see Ibarra, various).

9.7.1 How to reflect

The book 'How we think' by educator and philosopher John Dewey (1933 [1986]) is often cited as the seminal work on reflection. He is seen as a pioneer in advocating the role of reflection in learning. His ideas inspired many other important authors within the fields of psychology, education, organisational behaviour, and management (e.g., Kolb, 1984; Schön, 1983). The importance of reflection is further echoed by many more authors in a variety of disciplines informing our personal leadership model. We can go further and say that the ability to engage in critical reflection is one of the main differentiators between us and AI large language models. This is because reflective practice taps into the complex thinking processes which are inherently human.

While the case for reflective practice is clear, how to incorporate it in our day-to-day experiences to help us continue developing is less so. This is what Samuel found. During a leadership programme, Samuel was astonished to find that self-awareness was considered an important quality of leadership. He initially felt uncomfortable with the personal reflective exercises and assignments which formed part of the coursework. The first few times he was assigned to write about himself, he couldn't do it. What went on the page didn't feel natural. But he was intrigued by the notion of journaling and made a pact with himself to try to keep a journal for a year. He lay down some ground rules – it was for his eyes only, so no fretting about what he wrote or trying to make it interesting or readable. Also, he would try to write most days but would not feel guilty on those days where he couldn't or didn't.

Samuel has been amazed at the way in which a very small act – writing in a journal for 10 minutes a day – has had profound effects on his self-awareness and ultimately on his self-esteem. He feels more in tune with his values and priorities, and people have commented on his increased empathy. He also feels a bit more in control of his decisions and actions. It's too early to know whether it will make him a great leader, but Samuel is quietly happy with his experiment journaling his reflections and hopes to continue with it once the year is out. Of course, there is much more to reflection than frequent journaling. How to use a reflection is as important as committing to doing it. Donald Schön (1983) introduced two main ideas popularised in leadership development and organisation learning: 'reflection-on-action' and 'reflection-in-action'.

Reflection-on-action occurs after a particular situation, as individuals reflect on their experiences and actions, seeking to understand the underlying assumptions that guided their actions. So, it is important that the reflection method here includes a separation between facts, thoughts and feelings (including assumptions and biases) before an evaluative conclusion is reached. This process helps us to learn from our experiences with a bit of hindsight. It helps us to refine our skills, tweak our approach and improve the effectiveness of our actions over time. The main pitfall here is using post-event reflection as a stream of thought only, or to vent our frustrations. Releasing our emotions on paper is a very good process and advisable in other contexts; however, this is not exactly reflective practice on action. More importantly, reflection is not rumination, the process of going over and over a particular event or thoughts in a negative spiral without achieving a resolution. Rumination, like thinking errors, can be a sign of a deeper issue if they start being a frequent occurrence. If this is how you feel, we suggest seeking the help of a mental health professional, as this may be a sign something needs unpacking.

Reflection-in-action occurs in real time, while action is taking place. Individuals can adapt and adjust their actions in the moment, based on their ongoing observations and understanding of the situation. While this type of reflection can be useful, it may not be the most effective in situations when we are in the liminality of recalibration. As we are trying out different experiments, reflection-in-action can easily derail into something a bit more overcritical. This self-critic is something that individuals experiencing impostor syndrome often report and it can drain our psychological resources quite rapidly. If this is the case for you, a bit of self-compassion tends to be very effective in quieting this negative voice (see Papworth, 2023). Reflection-in-action, however, can be very valuable in terms of noticing, thus absorbing what is happening around and to us without rushing to judge or react. This 'information' when intentionally captured can be extremely insightful to understand what is going on with us in later reflections.

In addition to these two types of reflection proposed by Schön, we argue that reflection for action is also important. Gaining greater self-awareness and contextual awareness, as well as understanding our priorities and resources through reflection, is an essential preparation for intentional action. Not surprisingly, this is the basis of our model. This doesn't mean that we don't believe in spontaneous actions, these can generate surprisingly positive results. But they can also be time and energy consuming. Given that most people we meet in our workshops and life in general are overstretched, we advocate that a bit of thought goes a long way in preserving our precious resources. The only caveat here is not to get stuck in 'analysis paralysis'. It is important to know when to move on from reflection to action and experimentation.

9.8 The bottom line

In this chapter, we focused on experimentation encompassing action and reflection. These two elements were combined in this chapter due to the interconnected nature of these two processes for personal leadership development. We introduced different types of experiments, possible scenarios, and conditions for explorations of developing identities. We also explored several examples of experimentation, demonstrating how different individuals approach thinking and action. We concluded the chapter with a few points about reflection. While this is the last element of our model, it is not the end. Personal leadership is an iterative process and it may involve many cycles of recalibration. This recalibration may never end, as we are always in flux, and may follow a different sequence than we introduced here depending on the circumstances. In the next chapter we will explore the question 'what next' and highlight the key takeaways from this personal leadership journey.

Chapter 10
Personal leadership for life

In the previous chapters we covered different aspects of our sustainable personal leadership model, and gave you some tools for utilising the model to gain personal insight and implement changes to make the most of your longevity and engaged retirement. Any model is, at its heart, merely an invitation to view things from a particular perspective with the hopes that it will give you a richer picture, provide some answers, and some food for thought. To conclude this book, we will go back to the beginning and ask: What lies underneath the model? What else is there for you moving forward? Why did we feel compelled to write this book?

10.1 Leading Self, Inc.

This book is based on three propositions. The first is that increased longevity, combined with cultural, financial, and societal pressures, are fundamentally changing the nature of work, hence the rise of 'the age of no retirement' movement (Collie, 2015). This does not mean working till the day you die because there are no other options; it means that our mid and late life now encompass so many different potential paths that the term 'retirement' becomes even more meaningless. This takes us to our second and third propositions, namely, that each of us can prepare ourselves for this new age by making smart decisions. And that these decisions are, at their heart, leadership decisions.

This last is because, at the most basic level, we are the leaders of our own selves. And while we cannot predict the future and cannot control many of the things which happen to us, we can make decisions that allow us to be prepared, to be resilient, and to protect our well-being so that we can lead longer, healthier working lives. Whether you find this idea exciting or challenging, we will have shown you that it is possible to exercise good personal leadership as we age. While both of us, with our educators' hat on, believe these principles can be taught to young adults, we know that at midlife we have an advantage. Because by this point, we have accumulated a wealth of knowledge about ourselves and the world around us. We just need to know where to look for this wisdom and take the driving seat of our lives.

The fact you are reading this book means you are already on this journey. You may have already realised that you want to make changes, and that you have agency to do so. You may have just started to explore your priorities, goals and realities, or you may be ready to take this conversation deeper, to start real-life exploration of these nascent ideas inhabiting your head. You may have not known until now that this is leadership. And just like in an organisation, we need both the 'hard and soft' aspects of leadership, such as analysing the product and market, having a vision, a

https://doi.org/10.1515/9783111316147-010

strategy, and a contingency plan, while fostering psychological safety, a learning mindset, engagement, well-being and fulfilment. We are, after all, the CEO of Self, Inc.

10.2 Sustainable personal leadership is learning

Our model is based on three components – purpose, alignment, and experimentation. These are not exclusive, separate stages in a linear process, but rather, each feeds into the other in an iterative loop. So, although we offered a starting point, and have created some steps, we expect that your own needs and insights will show you where you should (re)visit. Above all, it is only by revisiting questions, dilemmas, assumptions multiple times and with fresh perspectives that we can start gaining insights. Therefore, sustainable personal leadership may be compared to navigating a labyrinth; there may be many entries and exits and we may have to come back to certain points a few times before trying different paths. As you gain these insights, you are learning and growing. And when you learn something new, about yourself, about the world, you can no longer ignore it. There is no going back from what we learn.

Learning entails much more than knowledge or education. Learning is what makes us, humans, adaptable. It is what allowed us to survive in the savannah, protect ourselves, build communities, etc. Learning complements biological evolution and enables us to go beyond surviving, but also thriving. Despite the myths around ageing and intelligence, we never stop learning. For most people, intelligence continues to develop into old age; we also tend to become better at managing our emotions, dealing with others' emotions, managing problems, and accepting the things we cannot change – instead focusing on what we can. We gain perspective as we age, and are able to see patterns that may have escaped us earlier. We can see cycles, and anticipate change – maybe not the specific change but the inevitability of it. This means we can become better at leading ourselves.

In case we haven't made it clear: personal leadership is all about learning, and learning never ends. As adults, we learn differently than as children, as we have a rich body of experience to draw on as we discover and experiment and reflect. This engaged learning process is not a rote process – not like memorising – but is a highly creative process. Unfortunately, we don't get much practice at the kind of creative experimentation that allows innovation to flourish. Many of you may feel that the type of reflective thinking and action we discuss in this book is hard work. But it is also deeply creative. For example, while there is work involved in examining your inner narrative and investigating the unconscious framing you might be using, there is a kind of joyful creativity in adopting a different frame. Our sustained personal leadership model encourages us to be creative, especially in the experimentation stage, but also through the exploratory processes of purpose and alignment.

As adults, we often tend to think in a very linear and goal-oriented way. While there is nothing wrong with goals, they are rarely achieved in the linear fashion we imagine, and in fact the process of iteration – recalibration as we have termed it herein – combined with false starts and left turns and unexpected twists, is a surprisingly effective way to navigate your path. In the first instance being creative involves being open to see multiple perspectives and to imagine multiple outcomes. It is deeply tied into being curious. So many of us have learned to associate creativity with risk, and therefore to be afraid of it.

We would be happy if one of the things you take away from this book is that being creative is not scary. Things may not always work out as expected, that is why we call it learning. You can take steps to minimise risk, if that makes you more comfortable, but to eliminate creativity because of risk would be a very sad way to live. Some people believe that creativity is an inherent part, or not, of your character. In other words, you either have it or you don't. But like so many other things, creativity is like a muscle, the more you use it the stronger it grows. As much as we'd like to give a recipe book to our readers, this is not a recipe book. If we change our analogy from cooking to theatre; we're not giving you a script on how to move forward, instead our intent is to give you something more akin to preparation notes for an 'improv' session. So that when an opportunity comes along, you can jump up and grab it. We recognise that when you are stuck, it is easy to feel paralysed and not know how to take the first step. That is why the model is there. As you reflect and recalibrate, remember that you can do things in stages. You don't need to have a grand solution or grand purpose. It is enough to take small steps. Equally, you may opt to take big, crazy steps. Ultimately, it is about ownership, because you are the CEO of Self, Inc., and its well-being is maintained through your leadership decisions.

10.3 Living with no regrets

While this book is aimed primarily at those in midlife, it has been designed to be helpful at any stage of adulthood. Thus, it should be useful to the 40-year-old thinking about a midlife career shift, to the 50-year-old wanting to shake things up, to the 60-year-old thinking about options for giving back, and to the 75-year-old thinking about what to do next. There is no standard template anymore for when you can change directions, for when to step off the fast road, or when to step back on it. We have encountered so many stories of people who have embraced change at all ages, from a change in perspective or framing to a radical shift in direction. Nevertheless, for many of us, there is still a strong urge to buy into the out-dated narrative that you have to be young to make a change or try something daring, like launching a start-up or travelling the world. We don't believe this narrative; we have accumulated enough research evidence and real-life examples to dispute its validity. Therefore, we are saying that you should not settle because you believe a societally imposed cost-benefit analysis on age and investment in self. It's never too late to invest in yourself. It's only too late when you are dead.

Fixed age-bound ideas exist hand-in-hand with ageism and the narrative of decline. These attitudes so often lead to regret and bitterness in late life. We haven't explicitly addressed regret in our model. Regret can impact terribly on our well-being and mental health. Too often, we regret things we didn't have the courage to do, paths we might have taken. Tatiana found during her Ph.D. that many informants regretted not spending more time with their children, being too focused on work, not exercising enough. So, regret can be palpable but avoiding it is not a good place to start our journey to personal leadership development.

Freud famously talked about two basic instincts driving human behaviour, which in simple terms can be described as 'seeking pleasure' and 'avoiding pain'. Using potential regret as a 'stick', rather than opportunities for fulfilment as a 'carrot' is not an approach that we underscore. Because, while some behavioural scientists claim that avoiding loss is a greater motivator than earning/winning something – often it does also lead to more mediocre solutions, poor creativity, and lack of innovation. This has been demonstrated in many studies which informed some suggested approaches in previous chapters (see Boyatiz' intentional change theory in Chapter 8 and the miracle question in Chapter 9). Therefore, we favour a more positive and fertile route to approach change and recalibration in midlife.

We also believe that regret, when it happens, should be processed in a way that increases our agency (not in a way that makes us helpless – remember the narratives and frames we discussed in Chapters 4 and 5). Therefore, by engaging in periodic reflection and recalibration of our priorities, goals, resources, we can also take out and examine regrets and let them go. Sometimes we are our own worst enemies when it comes to allowing ourselves to be happy. Life is as much about gains as it is about losses, and letting go is an important part of moving forward. Understanding ourselves, learning from our trials and errors, and engaging in self-compassion can help us to not become subsumed with what-ifs about the past. It is important that we carry on refreshing and moving forward.

10.4 From personal leadership to leadership

One aspect of leadership is developing others. In this book we have tried to show you how to be a smart and effective leader of your own story. However, none of us live in isolation. Some of our most powerful resources come from our social networks, from our relationships with friends, family, colleagues, and communities. In Chapter 8, we urged you to nurture these connections, and to give back to others, for example, to sit on the personal boards of others, providing sound guidance, honesty, cheerleading and perspective. Because, in the end, we are social animals and need belonging and community to flourish – even if discourses at work and society lead us to believe otherwise.

In our own work environment, we may be in a position to help others to engage in this process of recalibration. As we learn more about ourselves, we become more attuned to signs of stuckness in others. We may, therefore, be able to help them to start their journey to recalibration. By helping others to develop, learn and grow, your effective personal leadership skills boost your effectiveness as a leader in general. We have made the point here repeatedly that sustainable personal leadership is about making smart leadership decisions about Self, Inc. It makes sense that once you understand this analogy between leading a business and leading yourself, the skills that you acquire in one of these will affect the other as well.

Personal leadership has a ripple effect. As we take agency and ownership over our own paths through midlife and beyond, we create healthier options for ourselves. This benefits not only ourselves, but those around us, and our communities in general. Therefore, it is a misconception that personal leadership is only about ourselves; in reality it only starts with us but its reach is far. As we change our own attitudes, and increase our options for engaged and healthy working lives as we age, our experiences and decisions make an impact on those around us, in our workplaces, our communities, and our storytelling.

It was not too long ago that we humans invented the concept of retirement, and began to expect a standardised progression from education to employment to retirement as both a right and a norm. Now we have the opportunity to change that expectation to one where choices exist, and where we can continue to learn and grow and interact as we see fit, in whatever form that might take. It is up to us.

References

American Association of Retired Persons [AARP]. (2020), *Growing with Age. Unlocking the power of the multigenerational workforce*, Living, Learning, and Earning Longer Learning Collaborative Resources. Available at: https://www.aarpinternational.org/growingwithage

Arthur M. B., & Rousseau D. M. (1996). A career lexicon for the 21st century. *Academy of Management Perspectives*, 10(4), 28–39.

Arthur, M. B., Khapova, S.N., & Wilderom, C. P. M. (2005), Career success in a boundaryless career world. *Journal of Organizational Behaviour*, 26, 177–202.

Ashforth, B. E. (2001). *Role transitions in organizational life: An identity-based perspective*. Mahwah, NJ: Lawrence Erlbaum Associates.

Atchley, R. C. (1989). A Continuity Theory of Normal Aging. *The Gerontologist*, 29(2), 183–90.

Atchley, R. C. (1999; 2000). *Continuity and Adaptation in Aging: Creating Positive Experiences*. Baltimore, MD: The Johns Hopkins University Press.

Baltes, P. B., & Baltes, M. M. (1990). Psychological perspectives on successful ageing The model of selective optimization with compensation. In P. B. Baltes & M. M. Baltes (Eds.), *Successful aging: Perspectives from the behavioural sciences* (pp. 1–34). New York, NY: Cambridge University Press. Chapter 1.

Best, F. (1980). *Flexible life scheduling*. New York, NY: Praegar

Boyatzis, R. E. (2006). An overview of intentional change from a complexity perspective. *Journal of Management Development*, 25(7), 607–623.

Bridges, W. (1980). *Transitions. Making sense of Life's Changes*. Cambridge: Perseus Books.

Brown, A. D. (2015). Identities and identity work in organizations. *International Journal of Management Reviews*, 17(1), 20–40. doi:10.1111/ijmr.12035

Cambridge University Press. (n.d.). Recalibration. *In Cambridge Dictionary* [Online]. Retrieved June 21st, 2024, from https://dictionary.cambridge.org/dictionary/english/recalibration

Cain, S. (2013). *Quiet: The power of introverts in a world that can't stop talking*. New York: Broadway Paperbacks.

Carstensen, L. L. (2006). The influence of a sense of time on human development. *Science*, 312(5782), 1913–1915.

Cattell, R. B. (1971). *Abilities: their structure, growth, and action*. Boston: Houghton Mifflin.

Centre for Ageing Better (2018) *Age is just a number: Views among people aged 50 and over in the English Longitudinal Study of Ageing*. Available at: https://ageing-better.org.uk/sites/default/files/2018-11/ELSA-analysis.pdf

Charles, S. T., & Carstensen, L. L. (2010). Social and emotional aging. *Annual Review of Psychology*, 61, 383–409.

Collie, J. (2015). The Age of No Retirement. *Working with Older People*, 19(4), 159–164.

Dalton, C. (2021). *The Integrated Leader: A Foundation for Lifelong Management Learning*. New Jersey, London, Singapore, Beijing, Shanghai, Hong Kong, Taipei, Chennai, Tokyo: World Scientific Publishing Co Pte Ltd.

Dannefer, D. (2020; 2018). Systemic and reflexive: Foundations of cumulative Dis/Advantage and life-course processes. *The Journals of Gerontology. Series B, Psychological Sciences and Social Sciences*, 75(6), 1249–1263. https://doi.org/10.1093/geronb/gby118

De Vos, A., Van der Heijden, B. I. J. M., & Akkermans, J. (2020). Sustainable careers: Towards a conceptual model. *Journal of Vocational Behavior*, 117, 103196.

Denyer, K., & Rowson, T. S. (2022) "I've finally got my expression": the anchoring role of identity in changing from an organisation-based career to a protean career path. *British Journal of Guidance & Counselling*, 52(3), 367–377.

Dewey, J (1933[1986]). *How we think: A restatement of the relation of reflective thinking in the educative process*, In J.A. Boydston (Ed.), *Later works 8*. Carbondale and Edwardsville: Southern Illinois University Press.

Duffy, R. D., Spurk, D., Perez, G., Kim, H. J., & Rosa, A. D. (2022). A latent profile analysis of perceiving and living a calling. *Journal of Vocational Behavior*, 134, 103694.

Epstein, S. (1994). Integration of the cognitive and the psychodynamic unconscious. *American psychologist*, 49(8), 709.

Erikson, E. H. (1980). *Identity and the life cycle*. New York, London: W. W. Norton & Co.

Erikson, E. H. (1985). *The life cycle completed: A review*. New York, London: W. W. Norton & Co.

Featherstone, M. and Hepworth M., M in Featherstone, M., Hepworth, M. and Turner, B., (Eds.) (1991) *The Body*. London: Sage.

Ferraro, K., & Morton, P. (2018). What Do We Mean by Accumulation? Advancing Conceptual Precision for a Core Idea in Gerontology. *Journals of Gerontology Series B: Social Sciences*, 73(2), 269–278.

Freund, A. M., & Ritter, J. O. (2009). Midlife crisis: A debate. *Gerontology*, 55(5), 582–591.

George, M. M., Wittman, S., & Rockmann, K. W. (2021). Transitioning the study of role transitions: From an attribute-based to an experience-based approach. *Academy of Management Annals*, 16 (1), 102–133.

Giddens, A., (2001, [1991c]) *Modernity and Self Identity*. Cambridge: Polity

Gilleard, C. J., & Higgs, P. (2005). *Contexts of ageing class, cohort, and community*. Cambridge: Polity.

Gordon, J., Beatty, J., & Whelan-Berry, K. (2002). The mid-life transition of professional women with children. *Women In Management Review*, 17, 328–341.

Graeber, D. (2018). *Bullshit Jobs: A Theory*. New York, London, Toronto, Sydney, New Delhi: Simon & Schuster.

Graebner, W. (1980). *A history of retirement, 1885–1978*. New Haven/London, CT: Yale University Press.

Gratton L, Scott A. (2016). *The 100-Year Life: Living and Working in an Age of Longevity* New York: Bloomsbury Inf.

Hal, D. T. (1996). Protean careers of the 21st century. *Academy of Management Perspectives*, 10(4), 8–16.

Hall, D. T. (2004). The protean career: A quarter-century journey. *Journal of Vocational Behavior*, 65(1), 1–13.

Hayes, J. (2019), *Can you have it all? Women's transition to a leadership identity in professional services*. MSc Coaching and Behavioural Change Dissertation. Henley Business School. University of Reading, UK.

Hirschi, A. (2012). The career resources model: An integrative framework for career counsellors. *British Journal of Guidance & Counselling*, 40(4), 369–383.

Hirschi, A., Keller, A. C., & Spurk, D. (2019). Calling as a double-edged sword for work-nonwork enrichment and conflict among older workers. *Journal of Vocational Behavior*, 114, 100–111.

Hobfoll, S. E. (1989). Conservation of resources: A new attempt at conceptualizing stress. *American Psychologist*, 44(3), 513–524.

Horn, J. L. (1989). Models of intelligence. In R. L. Linn (Ed.), *Intelligence: Measurement, theory, and public policy: Proceedings of a symposium in honor of Lloyd G. Humphreys* (pp. 29–73). University of Illinois Press.

Ibarra, H. (1999). Provisional selves: Experimenting with image and identity in professional adaptation. *Administrative Science Quarterly*, 44(4), 764–791.

Ibarra, H. (2003). *Working identity: Unconventional strategies for reinventing your career*. Boston, MA: Harvard Business School Press.

Ibarra, H. (2007). *Identity Transitions: Possible Selves, Liminality and the Dynamics of Voluntary Career Change*. Fontainebleau, France: INSEAD Working Paper 2007/31/OB.

Ibarra, H. (2023). *Working Identity, Updated Edition, with a New Preface: Unconventional Strategies for Reinventing Your Career*. Harvard Business Press.

Ibarra, H., & Petriglieri, J. L. (2010). Identity work and play. *Journal of Organizational Change Management*, 23(1): 10–25.

Jones, R.J. (2020). *Coaching with research in mind*. Abingdon, Oxon: Routledge.

Jung, C. G. (1960). *The Structure and Dynamics of the Psyche*. Hove, New York: Routledge and Kegan Paul.

Kahneman, D. (2011). *Thinking, fast and slow*. London: Penguin Books

Kegan, R. (1982). *The Evolving Self: Problem and process in human development*. London: Harvard University Press.

Kegan, R. (1995). *In over our heads: The mental demands of modern life*. Cambridge, London: Harvard University Press.

Kegan, R., & Lahey, L. L. (2009). *Immunity to change*. Boston: Harvard Business Review Press.

Kluckhohn, C. (1951). Values and value-orientations in the theory of action: An exploration in definition and classification. In *Toward a general theory of action* (pp. 388–433). Cambridge: Harvard University Press.

Kolb, D.A. (1984). *Experiential Learning: experience as the source of learning and development*. New Jersey: Prentice Hall.

Kooij, D. T. A. M. (2015). Successful aging at work: The active role of employees. *Work, Aging and Retirement*, 1, 309–319.

Kuhn, M. H., & McPartland, T. S. (1954). An Empirical Investigation of Self-Attitudes. *American Sociological Review*, 19(1), 68–76.

Künemund, H., & Kolland, F. (2007). Work and retirement. In Bond, J. et al. (Eds). *Ageing in Society: European Perspectives on Gerontology*. London, Los Angeles, New Delhi, Singapore: Sage Publications. pp. 167–185.

Lachman, M. E., Teshale, S., & Agrigoroaei, S. (2015; 2014). Midlife as a pivotal period in the life course: Balancing growth and decline at the crossroads of youth and old age. *International Journal of Behavioral Development*, 39(1), 20–31.

Levinson, D., (1978; 1996) *The Seasons of a Man's Life*. New York: Alfred. A Knopf.

Luthans F., Avolio B., Avey J. B., & Norman S. M. (2007). Positive psychological capital: Measurement and relationship with performance and satisfaction. *Personnel Psychology*, 60(3), 541–572.

McAdams, D. P., & McLean, K. C. (2013). Narrative Identity. *Current Directions in Psychological Science*, 22(3), 233–238.

McAdams, D. P. (2018). Narrative Identity: What Is It? What Does It Do? How Do You Measure It? *Imagination, Cognition and Personality*. 37, 359–372.

Moghimi, D., Zacher, H., Scheibe, S., & Van Yperen, N. W. (2017). The selection, optimization, and compensation model in the work context: A systematic review and meta-analysis of two decades of research. *Journal of Organizational Behavior*, 38, 247–275.

Müller, A., Angerer, P., Becker, A., Gantner, M., Gündel, H., Heiden, B., Herbig, B., Herbst, K., Poppe, F., Schmook, R., & Maatouk, I. (2018). Bringing Successful Aging Theories to Occupational Practice: Is Selective Optimization with Compensation Trainable? *Work, Aging and Retirement*, 4(2), 161–174.

Organisation for Economic Co-operation and Development [OECD] (2020), *Promoting an Age-Inclusive Workforce: Living, Learning and Earning Longer*, OECD Publishing, Paris, Available at: https://doi.org/10.1787/59752153-en

Organisation for Economic Co-operation and Development [OECD] (2023), *Retaining Talent at All Ages*, Ageing and Employment Policies, OECD Publishing, Paris, Available at: https://doi.org/10.1787/00dbdd06-en

Papworth, K. D. (2023). *Compassionate Leadership: For Individual and Organisational Change*. Volume 4 of De Gruyter Transformative Thinking and Practice of Leadership and Its Development. Boston/Berlin: Walter de Gruyter.

Peseschkian, H., & Remmers, A. (2020). Life Balance with Positive Psychotherapy. In Messias, E., Peseschkian, H., Cagande, C. (Eds.) *Positive Psychiatry, Psychotherapy and Psychology*. Springer, Cham. https://doi.org/10.1007/978-3-030-33264-8_8

Phillipson, C., & Smith, A. (2005). *Extending the working life: A review of the research literature*. Department of Work and Pensions. Research Report No. 299. Available at: https://webarchive.nationalarchives.gov.uk/ukgwa/20100208134426/http://research.dwp.gov.uk/asd/asd5/agepositive.asp

Phillipson, C. (1990). The Sociology of Retirement. In Bond, J., Coleman, P. & Peace, S. (Eds.), *Ageing and Society: an introduction to social gerontology*. London: Sage Publications. pp. 144–160.

Phillipson, C. (2002). *Transitions from work to retirement*. Bristol: The Policy Press for the Joseph Rowntree Foundation.

Puhakka, P. (2022). *Becoming self-employed after the age of 50 – an IPA study of self-employed identity formation*. MSc Coaching and Behavioural Change Dissertation. Henley Business School. University of Reading, UK.

Rodrigues, R., Guest, D., & Budjanovcanin, A. (2013). From anchors to orientations: Towards a contemporary theory of career preferences. *Journal of Vocational Behavior*, 83(2), 142–152.

Rowson, T. S., & Phillipson, C. (2020). 'I never really left the university:' Continuity amongst male academics in the transition from work to retirement. *Journal of Aging Studies*, 53, 100853–100853.

Rowson, T. S., Jaworska, S., & Gibas, I. (2023). Hot topic: Examining discursive representations of menopause and work in the British media. *Gender, Work, and Organization*, 30(6), 1903–1921.

Rowson, T. S., Meyer, A., & Houldsworth, E. (2022). Work Identity Pause and Reactivation: A Study of Cross-Domain Identity Transitions of Trailing Wives in Dubai. *Work, Employment and Society*, 36(2), 235–252.

Savickas, M.L., Nota, L., Rossier, J., Dauwalder, J.-P., Duarte, M.E., Guichard, J., Soresi, S., Van Esbroeck, R., & Vianen, A.E.M. van (2009). Life designing: A paradigm for career construction in the 21st century. *Journal of vocational behavior*, 75(3), 239–250.

Savickas, M. L. (2020) Career construction theory and counseling model. In R. W. Lent & S. D. Brown (Eds.), *Career development and counseling: Putting theory and research into work*. Hoboken, NJ: Wiley, pp. 165–200.

Schein, Edgar H. (1990). *Career Anchors (discovering your real values)*. San Francisco: Jossey-Bass Pfeiffer.

Schön, D.A. (1983). T*he reflective practitioner: how professionals think in action*. New York: Basic Books.

Schurman, B. (2022). *The Super Age: Decoding Our Demographic Destiny*. New York, NY: Harper Business, an imprint of HarperCollins Publishing.

Sheehy, G. (1995). *New passages: mapping your life across time*. New York: Random House.

Snow, D. A., & Anderson, L. (1987). Identity Work among The Homeless: The Verbal Construction and Avowal of Personal Identities. *American Journal of Sociology*, 92, 1336–1371.

Swedberg, R. (2018). How to use Max Weber's ideal type in sociological analysis. *Journal of Classical Sociology*, 18(3), 181–196.

Tomlinson, J., Baird, M., Berg, P., & Cooper, R. (2018) Flexible careers across the life course: advancing theory, research and practice. *Human Relations*, 71 (1). pp. 4–22. ISSN 0018-7267

Tucker-Drob, E. M., Brandmaier, A. M., & Lindenberger, U. (2019). Coupled cognitive changes in adulthood: A meta-analysis. *Psychological Bulletin*, 145(3), 273–301.

United Nations [UN] Department of Economic and Social Affairs, Population Division (2022). *World Population Prospects 2022: Summary of Results*. UN DESA/POP/2022/TR/NO. 3. Available at: https://desapublications.un.org/publications/world-population-prospects-2022-summary-results

United Nations [UN] Department of Economic and Social Affairs, Population Division (2023). *World Social Report 2023: Leaving No One Behind In An Ageing World*. Available at: https://desapublications.un.org/publications/world-social-report-2023-leaving-no-one-behind-ageing-world

Watson, T. J. (2008). Managing Identity: Identity Work, Personal Predicaments and Structural Circumstances. *Organization*, 15(1), 121–143.

Wilson, T. (2011). *Redirect: The surprising new science of psychological change*. Penguin UK.

World Economic Forum [WEF] (2024). *Longevity Economy Principles: The Foundation for a Financially Resilient Future*. Insights Report, January 2024. In collaboration with Mercer. Available at: https://www.weforum.org/publications/longevity-economy-principles-the-foundation-for-a-financially-resilient-future/

World Health Organization [WHO] (2021). *Global report on ageism*. Geneva: World Health Organization; 2021. Licence: CC BY-NC-SA 3.0 IGO. Available at: https://www.un.org/development/desa/dspd/2021/03/global-report-on-ageism/

World Health Organization, [WHO]. (2002). *Active Aging: A Policy Framework*, Geneva.

Ybema, S., Keenoy, T., Oswick, C., Beverungen, A., Ellis, N., & Sabelis, I. (2009). Articulating Identities. *Human Relations*, 62, 299–322.

Zacher, H., & Froidevaux, A. (2021). Life stage, lifespan, and life course perspectives on vocational behavior and development: A theoretical framework, review, and research agenda. *Journal of Vocational Behavior, 126*, Article 103476.

List of figures

https://doi.org/10.1515/9783111316147-012

About the authors

Dr Tatiana S. Rowson is Associate Professor in Organisational Behaviour at Henley Business School. She teaches personal leadership development to students in the Henley MBA and undergraduate programmes. Tatiana is the Programme Area Director for Business and Management and is a member of the Henley Centre for Leadership. Her research interests encompass ageing, work, and employment, with a particular focus on how midlife transitions impact health, wellbeing, and economic activity in late career. Before joining academia, Tatiana worked as an organisational psychologist and executive coach for several high-profile organisations in the UK, Brazil, and the United Arab Emirates. She is currently based in the UK.

Dr Kelly Sloan is Associate Professor of Leadership at Henley Business School. She teaches personal leadership development to students in the Henley MBA programme and is a member of the Henley Centre for Leadership. Kelly leads a team which is responsible for student wellbeing and performance, and previously served as the Programme Director for the Henley MBA programmes. Before moving into management education, Kelly taught linguistics at universities in the US, Australia, and Germany. Having successfully pursued three separate careers, in two distinct academic fields and in management, she has first-hand knowledge of mid-career changes, which informs her research interests in career development at later life stages. Kelly is currently based in the UK.

https://doi.org/10.1515/9783111316147-013

About the series editor

Professor Dr Bernd Vogel is Professor in Leadership, Founding Director of Henley Centre for Leadership UK & Henley Centre for Leadership Africa, and Research Division Lead at the Department of Leadership, Organisations & Behaviour, University of Reading. He is a Visiting Professor at the University of Johannesburg and holds an Honorary Chair Professorship in Organizational Leadership, Woxsen University, India. Bernd received a Master's Degree in Business Administration and Economics and a PhD in Management from Leibniz University of Hannover. He was Lecturer at University of St. Gallen, Switzerland.

Bernd's interests span both academia and practice and he assists humans and organisations in life-long leadership learning journeys that help to develop and transform lives, organisations, and societal causes. He has been working for more than 25 years with global companies, business schools and universities.

His expertise focuses on strategic leadership to mobilise and maintain healthy organizational energy and performance; senior management teams; future of work and leadership; organization-wide leadership capability; followership; transformation, change and culture, and leadership development. Bernd has published in top-tier academic journals, has authored and edited several books, and contributes regularly to global media.

https://doi.org/10.1515/9783111316147-014

Index

https://doi.org/10.1515/9783111316147-015